Power Up Your
Confidence

Commu.

'Pa__ed from cover to cover with pr_ _.al things you can do to improve your confidence, and in work, as in life, confidence is everything. A book you can't afford to ignore.'

Kenneth Hambly MB, Bch, BAO, General Medical Practitioner

'Essential reading, especially in today's challenging and stressful society.'

Ann Burnett, writer and tutor

'This is terrific. A sensible guide for anyone needing to give their confidence a boost.'

Dr David Lewis, Chairman and Director of Research,
Mindlab International Ltd

'Packed full of easy-to-use gems, helpful hints, tips and observations to enhance your confidence at work and beyond.'

Ann McCracken, Managing Director, AMC2 and
Vice President, ISMAuk

'Powerful approaches that work – highly effective and well worth reading!'

Nicki Beveridge, Fellow CIPD, member ISMA,
business coach and HR consultant

Power Up Your Confidence

How to master the ultimate business skill

ALICE MUIR

Harlow, England • London • New York • Boston • San Francisco • Toronto • Sydney • Auckland • Singapore • Hong Kong
Tokyo • Seoul • Taipei • New Delhi • Cape Town • São Paulo • Mexico City • Madrid • Amsterdam • Munich • Paris • Milan

PEARSON EDUCATION LIMITED
Edinburgh Gate
Harlow CM20 2JE
United Kingdom
Tel: +44 (0)1279 623623
Web: www.pearson.com/uk

First published 2014 (print and electronic)

Pearson Education is not responsible for the content of third-party internet sites.

ISBN: 978-1-292-00260-6 (print)
   978-1-292-00283-5 (PDF)
   978-1-292-00282-8 (ePub)
   978-1-292-00834-9 (eText)

British Library Cataloguing-in-Publication Data
A catalogue record for the print edition is available from the British Library

Library of Congress Cataloging-in-Publication Data
Muir, Alice Jane.
 Power up your confidence : how to master the ultimate business skill / Alice Muir.
   pages cm
 Includes index.
 ISBN 978-1-292-00260-6 (print) -- ISBN 978-1-292-00283-5 (PDF) -- ISBN 978-1-292-00282-8 (ePub) -- ISBN 978-1-292-00834-9 (eText)
 1. Self-confidence. 2. Interpersonal communication. 3. Interpersonal relations. 4. Work--Psychological aspects. 5. Success in business. I. Title.
 BF575.S39M85 2014
 650.1--dc23
                          2013037944

10 9 8 7 6 5 4 3 2 1
17 16 15 14 13

Cover design by Two Associates

Print edition typeset in 10/15pt ITC Giovanni Std by 30
Printed and bound in Great Britain by Clays Ltd, Bungay, Suffolk

NOTE THAT ANY PAGE CROSS REFERENCES REFER TO THE PRINT EDITION

For Emma

Contents

About the author

Alice Muir is a Chartered Psychologist and an experienced teacher, trainer, author and life coach. She has worked as a lecturer and counsellor with the Open University, and has also run her own business for 20 years. Alice is a member of the British Psychological Society, the General Teaching Council and the Association for Coaching, and she is a Fellow of the International Stress Management Association (ISMA UK). She is also a wife and mother, with two grown-up children.

After coining the term *Stress Adviser* in 1994 Alice has trained hundreds of Stress Advisers all over the UK and overseas.

Alice has now published 12 books, mainly about stress and personal development, including *Coping with a Stressed Nervous System*, *Make Your Sensitivity Work for You* and *Overcoming Loneliness* (Sheldon Press) and, in the Hodder Education *Teach Yourself* series, *Relaxation Techniques*, *Beat Stress*, *Persuade Anyone with NLP* and *Overcome Depression*.

Alice is currently Features Editor on ISMA's journal *Stress News* and often provides 'expert comments' for many articles including those in *My Weekly*, *Psychologies*, *Prima*, *Mail on Sunday*, *The Herald* and *Essentials* magazine.

Acknowledgements

Many thanks to the following for giving information, motivation, support or time, in connection with the writing of this book:

Sallyanne Sweeney (Watson Little), Lynsey Briston (Customer Service Project and Content Controller), David N. Armstrong (Project Manager), Ayr Writers' Club, Scottish Association for Writers, Samantha Jackson (Commissioning Editor, Pearson), James Muir (retired Environmental Sponsor), Mariannette McKie (Office Manager), Colin Muir (Systems Developer), Catherine Armstrong (Development Analyst), Eloise Cook (Commissioning Editor, Pearson).

Introduction

I've found writing this book exciting. Exciting because it covers areas of self-confidence in the workplace not focused on before in one neat volume. And exciting because it pulls together so much of what I've learned about the importance of confidence in the workplace through coaching clients and supervising other coaches. There are so many tasks and situations that people hesitate to say they would like help with, for fear of appearing that they are not on top of the job.

The subject of confidence came on to my radar by accident, really. As a chartered psychologist and life coach facilitating workshops in a range of settings, the question of confidence was one that came up again and again, no matter what the main topic was. So coaching and training on presentation skills, stress management, public speaking, interview skills, negotiation, assertiveness, meeting and committee skills, and so many others would come down to confidence.

It's an unusual person who hasn't had concerns, and felt a lack of confidence, when starting a new job, giving their first presentation, giving a talk to a group of peers, moving up to management, or making a pitch to an important potential client. It's completely to be expected to feel a little apprehensive when attempting anything new, especially if it's important to us and our future success.

However, with stress levels and demands at work consistently high, and job security consistently low, being able to do your job more effectively and to worry less about it, has never been more important to your personal well-being. But also, if you, and your colleagues, can feel more confident at work, your performance will be more effective, and this will have these important broad-ranging implications and repercussions:

➡ There will be enhanced company productivity and quality of service.

➡ There will be more time and energy for staff creativity and innovation – and new ideas to develop the business and take it forward in fruitful directions.

➡ You will worry less about keeping your job.

➡ You will find work more satisfying and less stressful.

➡ Your health and well-being will improve.

➡ Your confidence will rub off on others, both colleagues and clients … a ripple in the pool effect.

➡ Friends and family will reap the benefits of all this when you're at home, too – because life isn't just about work.

Overall, your well-being, that of those around you, and also of your organisation, will improve. And I find it exciting that my background and experience as a trainer, coach, writer and chartered psychologist, has come together so usefully in writing this book. So, whatever it is you feel you want to deal with more confidently at work, you should find some effective and direct guidance here. No gimmicks, no flavour-of-the-week quick fixes. Just sound and sensible information and recommendations, gleaned from decades of experience helping people build confidence in these areas.

I want to show you the skills that will build and maintain your self-confidence, so that you're ready for any eventuality. That's why I've tried to create a book that will be a conveni-ent source of expertise long after you put it down for the first time. From presentations, to phone calls, to managing staff, whatever it is you want to deal with more confidently, you'll find straightforward approaches and know-how, as well as activities that you can use to discover more about yourself, and more about really helpful undemanding strategies that work. This book can sit on your bookshelf as a handy resource to dip into as your circumstances change, and you want to perform better on any unfamiliar situation that has arisen. Just like a manual for your car, I've created a self-confidence at work manual for you to put into practice now, and whenever you might need it in the days to come.

Life is 10 per cent what happens to you and 90 per cent how you react to it.

Charles Swindoll, American writer and speaker, b. 1934

How to use this book

→ **Terminology**. I've used the words client, company and workplace throughout as a cover-all for the many possible situations people work in, paid or unpaid. And 'line manager' is used to refer to the person or persons you report to (if you have one). This is simply to avoid clumsy text. I've also mixed the use of he and she all the way through.

→ **Take from the book what you want**. You can dip into chapters that interest you. Or you can read straight through from cover to cover. The content builds the more you read. So it's up to you.

→ **Get involved**. There are ideas and information to think about, techniques to try, and checklists and questionnaires to work on. And each chapter has lots of opportunities to become actively involved, signposted by these boxes: 'In action', 'In the zone', and 'Chill time'.

→ **You won't find overnight miracle cures here** – though there are some pretty fast fixes.

➡ **You'll find this book is a useful resource long after you put it down**. This is not a read it and leave it type of book. I've tried to create a book that you can come back to and flick through, as your circumstances change, and you feel the need to perform better on a new task.

➡ **This is a self-confidence at work manual for you**. You can keep it in a prominent place in the bookshelf, to use today, and any day, as and when it's needed.

➡ **Somewhere for notes**. It helps to have a small notebook and pencil or pen ready, or a netbook, laptop, or your mobile phone – whatever. Some different-coloured or shaped 'sticky pads' might come in useful, too. That way, you can make notes during activities, or just when you want to. Keep these notes somewhere safe, as they are just for you, a kind of 'personal journal'.

You'll find flexibility and tenacity, as well as confidence, in this book. Together, these will help you stay fit for purpose, with enhanced staying power and resilience. You'll be thinking ahead of the game, and ready for anything. That way, you'll be on top of your work, making it so much more satisfying for you, and for those around you. You'll also perform better, consistently, and still be able to enjoy life outside of the workplace.

Chapter one

Make confidence work for you

What you'll do in this chapter:	This will help you to be more confident in any work situation, especially:
1. Think about what confidence means to you.	1. Communication of all kinds and at all levels.
2. Find ways to build on your strengths.	2. Choosing your priorities and knowing your mind.
3. Think about what matters to you.	3. Decision making.
4. Discover that weaknesses are not all bad.	4. For any situation – feel calmer and more in control.
5. Discover how much you can do to add to self-confidence.	

Everyone has a comfort zone, at work and outside of it. When you're in your comfort zone, you're confident and at ease. You are in control. You perform well and get results. It's energising and rewarding. But, sometimes, you have to step outside that zone and its wrap-around security blanket. This can happen now and then, with lots of notice or unexpectedly, without even giving you the time to open your laptop.

That's where this book comes in. It will give you the means to extend your comfort zone, so that you won't have to step outside it again. Whatever the situation you want to deal with more confidently, there will be something here to help you. Each chapter will look in detail at the kinds of work situations many people would prefer to cope with much better, from making a pitch to facilitating a team meeting, from managing staff to video-conferencing with co-workers in other cities or other countries. And in each chapter you'll learn skills and techniques that will help you to improve your performance, whatever the situation. There will also be quick and easy ways to tackle those nerves, which often get in the way too.

Making a start

This first chapter will lay the foundations for the whole book. To make any headway in improving your self-confidence at work, you first have to really know yourself, your strengths, your weaknesses and what's important to you. You have to make sure you have a positive sense of your own identity. And you need to know how to appear calm and self-assured in any situation. There are no magic wands or special tricks, just sound and reliable common sense and easily grasped specific skills.

> *Sometimes we stare so long at the door that is closing, that we see too late the one that is open.*
>
> **Alexander Graham Bell, inventor of the telephone, 1847–1922**

Typical problem areas

Here are some of the typical situations that many people would like to deal with better and approach with more confidence. Can you pick out those with which you can identify? Are there others you would add?

You	You and other people
Making a presentation	Socialising with colleagues
Speaking up in a group	Being domineered or bullied
Giving a talk or report to a group	Managing colleagues who report to you
Coping with stress	
Being criticised or put down	Managing your team
Not being listened to	Dealing with authority figures
Taking things too personally	Raising awkward topics with others
A failure of some kind	
Dealing with change	Criticising others
Being too sensitive	Ensuring manager follow-through on promises
Moving beyond your comfort zone	Teleconferencing and videoconferencing
Using new high-tech equipment	An appraisal/an interview
Returning to work after a break	Contacting a department you don't know well
Changing demands	
Facilitating/chairing a meeting	Saying no to people
	Coping with conflict
	Dealing with a difficult manager or colleague
	Making an important phone call

What is a confident person?

The following diagram lists a few ideas of what a confident person behaves like, and how they think. The diagram represents a rounded individual, with confidence across a range of areas. Most people won't have this rounded shape, and will have areas where they have less confidence than others. Have a read through them. Which aspects do you tick already? And which do you feel you want to work on?

CONFIDENT PEOPLE

Themselves
Positive
Know how to relax
Care about themselves
Have respect for themselves
Are clear about their goals in life
Not afraid to ask for help or advice
Understand themselves and their needs
Are in control of themselves and their emotions
Are aware they have weaknesses and can admit to them
Are not afraid to show their feelings when it's appropriate
Have a solid feeling of self-worth which comes from inside
Activities
Are able to adapt and cope easily in a range of different situations
Have a range of skills, but will admit if a task is too difficult for them
Can be outgoing, or quiet and thoughtful, depending on the situation
Know they can get things wrong, and don't worry about this
Relationship with others
Can be angry, but can handle this in themselves and others too
Are able to compromise and know when they should do so
Enjoy socialising and spending time with other people
Will not criticise other people unfairly or needlessly
Can listen actively when other people are speaking
Treat others fairly, and don't put them down
Care for and have respect for other people
Can understand others and their needs
Planning and problem-solving
Problems don't overwhelm them
Know where they want to go
Ready to be flexible
Forward thinking
Calm

Can you be too confident?

What about being too confident? Is it possible to be too confident? No doubt you will have heard criticisms of others who are 'getting too big for their boots', or 'arrogant', and this might make you concerned about becoming confident at all, far less over-confident. All I can say here is that, when I talk about 'confidence', I'm talking about a quality best described by the list just given in the previous diagram. 'Over-confidence' is a term usually used in a critical sense, and most often in connection with the following behaviours, and this is certainly not what I want you to aim for.

I'm not aiming for you to become:

self-important

aggressive

arrogant

superior

selfish

vain

bossy

conceited

big-headed

over-confident

full of yourself

IN THE ZONE

Spend time with up-beat colleagues

Make a point of getting to know colleagues who are always optimistic, enthusiastic and quietly confident. It definitely rubs off.

What is important to you?

If you want to become more confident, even in just one or two small areas of your work, it can be beneficial to think about the bigger issues in life, and how important these are to you, so that you can put it all into context in your personal great scheme of things.

What to do

For the following list, give each item a score of 0, 1, 2, 3 or 4, as described in the box below. Note in your personal journal any for which you score a 3 or a 4. Choose the number that best fits how you rate the importance that item has for you. Don't think too deeply, your first thought is probably the most accurate. Think in terms of how important you feel each item is to you, in general, most of the time.

Subject area		
Adventure	Affection	Approval
Achievements	Being the best	Challenge
Creativity	Excitement	Enjoying life
Friends	Freedom	Having children
Having a partner	Helping others	Happiness
Integrity	Independence	Intimacy
Knowledge	Leadership	Learning
Love	Making your mark	Marriage
Money	Novelty	Property
Passion	Political beliefs	Power
Religious beliefs	Respected	Risk-taking
Security	Status	Success
Travel	Variety	Wealth
Winning	Your work	Your hobby
Your home	Your health	Your family

This does not matter to me at all	Not so important to me	Quite important to me	Very important to me	Extremely important to me
0	1	2	3	4

To think about

➡ Which are your lowest scores – 0s and 1s – what's least important to you?

➡ What about the highest scores? How many 4s? What are your highest scoring items?

➡ Thinking about the areas of work you would like to deal with more confidently, are any of your high or low scores connected to these in any way? (This isn't the case for everyone.)

You'll never solve problems using the same thinking you created them with.

Albert Einstein, theoretical physicist, 1879–1955

Less tension means more confidence

Some common tasks at work, maybe facilitating a meeting or contacting an important client, can make you feel a little tense, anxious or uncertain. These feelings can mean you perform less well because anxiety particularly affects your memory, how you deal with quick decisions, complex tasks such as mental arithmetic, and how articulate you are. It has much less effect on more physical tasks such as keyboard skills or filing.

That's why you'll find a box called 'Chill time' in every chapter. Each of these will contain a 'quick and easy' relaxation technique others have found helpful, so that you can try these out and find which works best for you. These reduce tension and anxiety, meaning you can be more confident in all your tasks. Earlier chapters such as this one, will give you ways of relaxing your body, and later chapters will concentrate on calming your mind.

This chapter will kick this off with a quick and easy relaxation technique for your body – at the end of this section.

But first, here is what makes 'Chill time' especially important for you:

1. It gives you a bit of a break from reading!
2. 'Quick and easy' relaxation techniques take seconds to do, and are especially good for calming you and helping you to think more clearly at work, whatever you're doing.
3. Chill time techniques are totally invisible to others, and can be done anywhere, any time. Or in any 'empty moments' such as in a lift, on an escalator, waiting for your laptop to fire up or something to print, stopped at traffic lights, in a queue, or during any break time.
4. To combat long-term stress, try using Chill time techniques several times a day.

Chill time

You'll get the best results by trying each Chill time technique once or twice to get a feel for it, then use any time you want.

Scanning

1. Take a long breath in and, as you do, silently scan your whole body, and notice if there is any muscle tension.
2. Then, as you breathe out slowly, relax any tension that you found.
3. Repeat 1 and 2 once or twice more, if needed.

Why weaknesses are not all bad

We all have strengths and weaknesses. It would be nice if everyone had no weaknesses but, we live in the real world, and everyone has weaknesses. The important idea is to be aware of our weaknesses, and take these into account in our lives without being weighed down by them. But, correspondingly, we should also try to be aware of our strengths, and build on these.

Here is a list of some common strengths. Look over the list and choose up to five of those that you would consider to be your main strengths. Or maybe there are some other strengths you feel you have which we have not listed. Make a note of these down the left-hand side of a new page in your journal. No modesty allowed. Go on, be honest!

Common strengths

Practical	Intuitive
Open-minded	Adventurous
Well organised	Clever
Understanding	Quick thinker
Explains things well	Good memory
Good at reading people	Copes in a crisis
Thoughtful of others	Reliable
Outgoing	Easy with people
Good with words	Copes under pressure
Hard-working	Creative with ideas
Good listener	Caring
Calm	Trustworthy
Perceptive	Imaginative
Good team player	Persistent
Patient	Sense of humour
Has ideas	Decisive

Now look over the next list of characteristics commonly viewed as weaknesses, and choose up to five of these that you would consider to be your main weaknesses (or maybe there are some other weaknesses you feel you have which we have not listed). Take a new page in your journal, and make a note of these down the left-hand side.

Common weaknesses

Self-centred

Sometimes uncaring

Aggressive

Slow worker

Sometimes cruel without realising it

Not punctual

Disorganised

Misses targets

Difficulty compromising

Hurtful

Dogmatic

No sense of humour

Sometimes deliberately cruel

Can't empathise with others

Untidy

Forgets to do things

Doesn't think things through

Impatient

No ideas

Inattentive

Not a good listener

Not a good planner

Rude

Manipulative

Unreliable

Jumps to conclusions

But there is also a much more positive note to the weaknesses we all have. And that positive note is that, for every weakness, you will have a corresponding strength. Sounds odd? The two go hand in hand, each the partner of the other. If you think about it, a colleague who is very passive may have a corresponding sensitivity that they would not otherwise have. An employee who isn't good at following instructions might be very creative and have good ideas. If your line manager talks too much it could be because they are very enthusiastic and keen to help. Let's think about this idea a bit more.

In action

Good things come in threes

At the end of each day, take a few moments to think back over the day. Write down three good or positive things that happened. No need to be anything major: a report completed on time, lunch with a friend, a compliment from a colleague. Start with every day to get the idea, then maybe three or four times a week. At the end of each week, read back over your list of positive features. Studies show this simple process can alter your mindset for the better, and improve your self-confidence.

Weaknesses are strengths, too

For each weakness you picked out earlier, and listed in your journal, try to find its more positive partner and write it beside it. There is always one! You can't have one without the other ... but it can sometimes take a bit of thinking time to work out what the corresponding strength is. Here are some more examples to give you the idea:

Weakness	Corresponding strength
Shy	Modest
Quiet in meetings	Good listener
A worrier	Thinks carefully about things
Too sensitive	Cares about other people's feelings
Slow worker	Pays good attention to detail
Lacks confidence in some tasks	Keen to be good at all tasks

As an optional extra, you could repeat this process, this time for your list of strengths, and think about their more negative partners. This can also throw up some useful outcomes for you, which may also be illuminating.

It's really getting down to basics when we put our strengths and weaknesses under the microscope like this. You can feel a bit exposed. But the process can be very revealing and very helpful. It can even help us to grow as people. Most importantly, it can help us to see our weaknesses in a completely different light, which has less of a draining effect on our confidence. And it does help when we are able to see the full picture and not just part of it.

The myth of perfect confidence

Perfect confidence is something of an illusion – nobody is completely confident all of the time and in every situation. And we all have good days and bad days, too. People have also become very good at hiding a lack of confidence, through excuses, bravado, avoidance and delegation. So don't be overly self-critical and don't make things too difficult for yourself. Making some headway on a few key points that matter most to you could be all you need to start with. You can then move onward when you're ready. You'll reap the rewards in day-to-day enhanced performance and improved health and well-being, as well as securing improvements in your long-term career path.

Problems are not stop signs, they are guidelines.

Robert H. Schuller, American motivational speaker, b. 1926

➡ Reading this book will show you how to expand your comfort zone at work.

➡ No one is 100 per cent confident, 100 per cent of the time. Everyone around you at work will have tasks they would prefer to carry out with more self-confidence. Either they hide this very well, or you've not noticed the signs (or don't know what they are).

➡ Keeping some easy-to-compile notes in a personal journal is a great confidence booster.

➡ Open your eyes to your achievements and strengths – use them and build on them.

➡ For every weakness you'll have a corresponding strength. Even being too sensitive has a positive side.

➡ There are simple and easy ways to keep nerves in check.

➡ It is really worth improving your self-confidence, as it will improve your career prospects, general health and well-being.

Chapter two

How to have a confident mindset

What you'll learn in this chapter:	This will help you to be more confident in any work situation, especially:
1. Thinking patterns that could be letting you down. 2. How to eliminate everyday beliefs that may be holding you back. 3. Ways to handle change and new demands. 4. Down-to-earth techniques that can improve performance.	1. Meetings of all kinds. 2. Presentations. 3. Planning your career path. 4. Forward planning. 5. Changing role. 6. Changing structure. 7. Changing demands. 8. Appraisals.

There are many normal patterns of thought and belief that can actually cause you to lack confidence in your own abilities. These everyday thoughts can relate to yourself, other people or life in general. This chapter will show you how to identify these thoughts, and stop them limiting your potential and creating self-doubt. This is easier than you may think, because these are commonplace thoughts, and how we think is not fixed and pre-set. Our thinking can be altered relatively easily. And, changing your thoughts is quite definitely within your control. I'll explain more, beginning with tracking down any 'unhelpful beliefs' you might have.

Parallel universes

I don't know the key to success, but the key to failure is trying to please everyone.

Bill Cosby, American actor, comedian and educator, b. 1937

These are many commonly held beliefs that are unhelpful and self-limiting because they are very fixed views. They can hold you back from achieving what you want in life, if you firmly believe them. Some are simply unhelpful, some are actually incorrect. Here are some very commonly held unhelpful beliefs about the world. Most people hold several of these. Do you believe any of these to be true?

1. I should be good at everything.
2. Life should be fair.
3. I need everyone to approve of what I do.
4. I shouldn't make a mistake.
5. Everyone is more important than me.
6. I have to be perfect.
7. People will reject me if I fail.

Most of these beliefs develop in childhood, picked up from those around us: parents, teachers, peer group, society in general. It's easy to see how holding any one of these beliefs very strongly can bring its own problems as you grow up. Believing you should never make a mistake and that you must have everyone's approval is destined for failure, but many people strive to achieve these aims day in day out. Small wonder this may cause a lack of self-confidence. And these are very deeply held points of view and assumptions, which we don't think of as 'beliefs'. We just hold these to be truths about us and our world, a kind of parallel reality.

But if you think it through carefully, beliefs 1–7 are unlikely to be the truth. Here is a more likely version of each of these beliefs:

	Mistaken belief ✗	Truth ✓
1.	I should be good at everything.	No one is good at everything. We all have strengths and weaknesses.
2.	Life should be fair.	Almost always life will be unfair at some point in our lives.
3.	I need everyone to approve of what I do.	You will rarely, if ever, please everyone. And you don't need to.
4.	I should never make a mistake.	Everyone makes mistakes. It's normal human behaviour.
5.	Everyone is better than me.	Everyone is equal, with equal rights.
6.	I have to be perfect.	Absolutely no one is perfect. It's just not possible.
7.	People will reject me if I fail.	Everyone fails sometimes. It doesn't mean you're a bad person.

If you recognise that you hold one or more of these beliefs, then just having this new information and awareness can feel like one of those 'light-bulb' moments, when something suddenly clicks, and you see there's another way of looking at it, another reality. Just like the picture of a vase that suddenly switches to a face. Or the old glass half empty or half full idea. And, as the new way of seeing the world usually feels much better, and gives you confidence instead of taking it away, then your life will have been changed instantly. You'll have been teleported to an alternative parallel universe without moving a muscle.

Flipping cube

Look at the cube below without looking away for up to 30 seconds or so. For most people it suddenly 'flips', and you seem to be looking at it in a different way. (If it doesn't work for you, see Appendix 2 for a hint.)

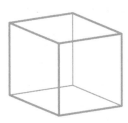

Positive self-talk

Just as some beliefs and thoughts that go through your head can pull your confidence down, there are other ways of thinking that do the opposite; they can lift you up and make you feel that you matter, that you have much to offer. Here are some short and simple phrases, sometimes called affirmations, which confirm a new more positive and optimistic way of seeing the world. It doesn't matter if you feel uncomfortable, or don't fully believe them at first, the more you think them, or write them down and glimpse their truth, the stronger your allegiance to them will become:

✓ I am a worthwhile person.

✓ I am an OK person.

✓ My feelings are real and important.

✓ I have many useful skills.

✓ I believe in myself.

✓ I matter.

✓ I have choices.

✓ My opinions matter.

Why too many changes and new demands can erode confidence

It is not the strongest of the species that survive, nor the most intelligent, but the one most responsive to change.

Charles Darwin, English naturalist, 1809–1882

Feeling a lack of confidence at work is often brought about by too much change and continually increasing demands, both of which are only too common in today's workplace. As recently as a few decades ago, work roles were more consistent and changes, if any, were well flagged up and slowly introduced. You could leave school, train for a job and then do that job till you retired. That was the norm for many decades up until around the 1980s. Working was in many ways more settled and predictable, and having self-confidence was relatively easy. Then everything changed totally. Largely for economic and global reasons, jobs for life disappeared, as a flexible and adaptable workforce became more and more what was needed in the industrialised countries.

The current mercuric workplace scenario was fully established by the end of the twentieth century. Everything could change in the blink of an eye. You might have a new curriculum to put straight into place, a hurriedly restructured workplace to get your head around, or a new set of regulations or working practices to take on board, and a new word, 'downsizing', came into your vocabulary. Staff would leave, and their workload just had to be covered. It's not surprising, then, to find that one of the major workplace stressors is frequent change, without time to properly assimilate it, and changing demands placed on you, without the time and resources to smooth these over. What this means is that those working today have had to learn skills of flexibility and adaptability fast, in order to survive in the workplace. Your grandparents never needed these. The settled, predictable working day experienced by almost every previous working generation has all but disappeared.

IN THE ZONE

Do something new and different

Make it something that really appeals to you. Make it a bit of a challenge. Anything will do. A new project at work, a sponsored run for charity, holiday somewhere special or learn a new language. The sense of achievement will energise and enthuse you.

We're all in it together

So, even though your colleagues may appear to be taking changing demands in their stride, everyone is actually in the same boat. Some are finding it easier than others mainly because of their personality and skill set or being more geographically mobile. Some people naturally find change and the stress it causes easier to cope with than others. Some skills are more transferable than others, making changing demands very much easier to take on seamlessly. Training in accountancy, project management or graphic design, for example, is much more transferable and adaptable than, say, dentistry or speech therapy. Being able to risk a change of job or a move elsewhere can be extremely difficult for many, particularly if they have caring responsibilities or are the sole breadwinner and would rather not take risks with their income. So, you can find yourself unable to move to a less demanding job and left with no option but to face increasing change and demands.

How was your day?

Each evening, or first thing the next morning, make a short note describing your day. Use a single word or phrase – good, OK, more positive today, disappointing or fair. Alternatively select a suitable 'smiley' (or 'emoticon') or simply score your day on 1 to 10 or 1 to 100. How you do this is entirely up to you. When you look back over these notes, they really help you to see where the good days and bad days were and, if cross-referenced with your work diary, they could even flag up reasons why. Sometimes this can show that you've had more good days than you thought. It's so easy only to remember the tough days.

How the bigger picture can change your outlook on life

I change my thoughts, I change my world.

Norman Vincent Peale, author of *The Power of Positive Thinking* (written in 1952 and still a bestseller), 1898–1993

Our grandparents and their parents, and all the way back to the Industrial Revolution over two centuries ago, didn't have to think in terms of change and increasing demands at all, so you've probably not had a role model for the mindset we all need today. Nobody has. As touched on already, jobs were pretty much for life, pre-1980. There was no real need for flexibility or adaptability. Before the Second World War, generation after generation of the same family worked at the same jobs, doing what their father or mother did, in the mines, cotton mills and other factories, in domestic service, agriculture, teaching or in heavy engineering. Hours were long and work was hard. Even if you had your own business, poverty and unemployment was such that your children would gladly follow in your footsteps, with company names such as 'Jones and Sons, Solicitors' commonplace. So, even as a growing child, you knew what your job was going to be as an adult, and it would be till you retired. For many this represented huge security, as the alternative may have been starvation and the workhouse. But, for others, knowing they had no choice but to spend their lives down a mine or in a menial job in a factory, must have been hugely dispiriting.

I mention all of this because, when you lack self-confidence at work, it helps to see your current employment situation in its long-term context and the product of external forces beyond your control and not just the outcome of your line manager's whims or your own shortcomings. It can help if you can see the bigger picture. Just like the wasp on your window trying desperately to find its way out, unaware that the open-ing, fresh air and freedom are but a few inches away. It helps because you can see that everyone around you has also found themselves in this situation through no choice of their own, and that most people lack confidence in their ability to cope, even though they are not saying so. But, there is so much you can do to make coping that much easier and, unlike the wasp, find the open window without a frenzied struggle.

Here are some key tips on how to approach the changing demands we all face today:

1. **Begin to think ahead of the game and outside the box.** This may seem like just another burden and so much more jargon, especially with everything else that is on your 'to do' list. But, if you take this on little by little, it will become a way of life and will not impact particularly on your to do list.

2. **Remember everyone is in the same boat, so it's not just you.** We are now living in changing times and uncharted waters. So share your experiences with others you can trust, colleagues or those outside your work circle. Approach someone who

seems quite similar to you, and copes well, and ask about their strategy. Or ask them to mentor you informally. It's becoming quite common for two people to organise reciprocal mentoring with each providing support to the other for a skill they have, so that there's more of a feeling of equality and reciprocity.

3. **Don't forget how the worldwide economic system contributes to your lack of confidence**. So, transfer some of the energy you're currently expending blaming yourself into understanding and managing the repercussions of this more effectively.

4. **Help yourself to more confidence**. The skills in this book will support you through changing demands, particularly:

    – how you can create the right mindset (this chapter);
    – recognising and building on your strengths (Chapter 1);
    – reinforcing your resilience to adversity (Chapter 7);
    – relaxing regularly, both mind and body ('Chill time' in every chapter);
    – ways to reach your goals and stay motivated (Chapter 8);
    – career-long confidence builders ('In the zone' in every chapter).

Chill time

Slow down

1. Sit comfortably and quietly.

2. Close your eyes gently (if you can) and become aware of your breathing. Take a gentle breath in and, in your own time, sigh it back out, allowing your shoulders to relax.

3. Now, in your own time, as you breathe in, silently place the word 'slow' on your inward breath and, as you breathe out, place the word 'down' on your outward breath.

4. Repeat this for one to two minutes.

Must you?

There is a monologue going on in our heads every day: 'This traffic is worse than usual', 'What will I cook for dinner tonight?', 'Bill wants a response by today'. But this inner voice of ours can sometimes include unhelpful words such as 'ought', 'should' or 'must'. Here are some examples to think about:

➡ I must phone Harry today.
➡ I must get that e-mail done today.
➡ I ought to learn more about that.
➡ I should have made a better job of that.

If you think about each of these inner thoughts, they are the result of self-imposed expectations and overly strict personal rules – and they are coming from yourself. Somewhere in your past, these will have been established in your mind, probably as a result of your interactions with someone else: a parent, teacher or a friend? But it's only you keeping them going now.

It's interesting for you to challenge these now by asking yourself questions such as, 'Why?' and 'Who says'? Naturally, if 'Who says?' is your line manager, that's a different story, but, that apart, this will help you to let these unhelpful personal rules go and adapt your thoughts to something more positive.

Unhelpful ✗	Questions to ask ?	Helpful ✓
I must phone Harry today.		I'd like to phone Harry today if I can.
I must get that e-mail done today.	Why? Who says?	It would be good if I can get that e-mail done today, but tomorrow would do.
I ought to learn more about that.		I'd like to learn more about that, if I can.
I should have made a better job of that.		I'd rather have done that better.

More unhelpful thinking habits

Most of us are not aware of it, but how our thinking developed as we grew up can be responsible for current difficulties. This section will introduce you to some of the most common thinking habits that can contribute to problems such as anxiety, stress or low self-confidence. For any particular situation, they cause us to ignore more positive, more likely, explanations in favour of negative explanations that are actually much less likely.

Have a look over these common thinking habits. Do any of these apply to you? Some of them are fairly close in meaning, so you may find a degree of overlap and crossover amongst them.

Thinking habit	What you might say	Your behaviour
Crystal ball gazing	It's a sign. It was meant to be. It's not meant to be.	Looking for signs of the 'right way' to go, instead of looking at it logically. Believing the future is set and you can't do anything to change it. But you can!
Catastrophising	It will be a disaster. I'll make a complete mess of it.	If something goes wrong, there's no way back and you think the whole project will fail completely. You have everything out of proportion.
Personalisation	It's all my fault. That's down to me. Sorry …	Always blaming yourself for anything negative that happens, with no justification. Whatever goes wrong or doesn't work out, you'll be sure you were responsible.
Thinking in extremes	I knew she would be nothing but trouble. That was a complete waste of time.	Fixed thinking. You see people or events only in extremes, good or bad, failure or success. Nothing in between. You can flip from one to the other for a minor reason.
Jumping to conclusions	That's it then. No need to wait for more feedback. It's back to the drawing board.	Use flimsy evidence to *reach a very negative conclusion*. Ignore more plausible explanations, for no good reason at all.

Thinking habit	What you might say	Your behaviour
Jumping to causes	No need to look any further, then. We've lost out because of John's weak pitch.	Use flimsy evidence to *decide on the cause of a very negative outcome*. Ignore more plausible explanations for no good reason at all.
Negative focus	That will never work. I wouldn't get your hopes up. That training session was another waste of time.	You focus completely on the negative, as if the positive side didn't matter at all. You ignore all the things that went well and let one negative feature dominate.

Creating your own flashbulb moments

For many people, just becoming aware of their unhelpful thinking habits, along with their negative effects, can establish long-lasting change – the 'flashbulb moment'. But, for others, it can take more than that. There is a very effective technique you can try that can substantially reduce the negative impact of these ways of thinking about the world.

So, if you have identified with any of the 'unhelpful' thoughts or beliefs in this chapter, but are finding it difficult to 'switch' to a more positive view, here is what you can do. For each of your unhelpful beliefs ask yourself the following seven questions – think them through, and answer them honestly. Use your personal journal to write your answers and other comments, or just think your way through this process.

1. What is the evidence to support this belief? Have my life experiences provided any evidence for it?

2. Who says it's true? Is it written down somewhere that this is true?

3. What effect does this belief have on my peace of mind, health and well-being?

4. Did I choose this belief for myself, or was it an outcome of my childhood experiences?

5. What would I tell a friend who believed this?

6. What would be a more realistic and positive belief?

7. Is there evidence supporting the alternative belief in the previous question?

DON'T FORGET

TABs

Taken together, I like to call thoughts (T), assumptions (A), and beliefs (B), that are unhelpful TABs for short.

Mindfulness boosts confidence

A skill that can make a life of change and constant demands easier to deal with is 'mindfulness'. This is one of those topics that has come on to the scene in a big way in a short space of time. And rightly so, because, for such a simple process, it has surprisingly powerful and far-reaching effects. It can create inner calm, harmony and a sense of empowerment, and so enhance confidence across the board.

But, in reality, mindfulness is not a new skill, but a very old one, which people across the world have used for hundreds of years when they wanted to feel more centred and at ease.

What's made the difference is that just in the last 20 years or so, researchers have been able to confirm that using mindfulness regularly can reduce tension, stress and anxiety and produce more calm. So what is this amazing technique?

Mindfulness can change your world

Using mindfulness to promote well-being and calm was first studied by Dr John Kabat-Zinn, emeritus Professor of Medicine at the University of Massachusetts, who began his work on the subject over 30 years ago. Mindfulness is not a complex technique nor is it attached to a belief system. In fact, it couldn't be simpler, it's simply a way of being. Yes, that sounds a bit out there, but it's not really. In fact, it couldn't be less so.

Our days are often spent ruminating in our heads about what happened last night, yesterday, or last month, or thinking ahead about what's next in our schedule today or targets not to miss tomorrow. So much so, that we can rarely spend time experiencing now.

Being mindful brings your mind from the past or from the future into the here and now, into this moment. And you absorb the detail of that moment. So, you're being mindful as you watch waves quietly lap up the shore onto the beach, listening to the sound and thinking of nothing else. Sitting quietly watching the countryside drift past on a long train journey is being mindful.

How people benefit from mindfulness

➡ Lateefa says: *'The phrase "get into the here and now" was so easy to follow, like a signpost. Without effort, and before I knew what had happened, I could do it. Here I was in the here and now, feeling as if I'd come to a sudden halt and was able to see clearly around myself for the first time in months.'*

➡ Daniel says: *'It was as if I had at last taken my foot off the accelerator pedal and my mind was no longer filled with the daily hurly burly. It was so much easier to plan, make decisions, find solutions and come up with new ideas.'*

➡ Ben says: *'I realised I had been spending too much of my time with my head in the future, but rarely in the here and now. What did I have to get done today and how I was going to manage it? What about that deadline? That meeting later? And that conference call? I feel so much better after spending just a minute in the here and now, slowly focusing on the world around me.'*

Easy ways to use mindfulness

Mindfulness is a way of being and a way of life that can provide a simple escape from endless hustle and bustle. It's often just described as coming into the 'here and now'. Even being mindful for just a minute several times each day has a marked calming effect on the mind and body, building resilience to stress or depression, and simplifying everything that your day expects of you. Here are a few ideas to get you started. Try these when there's a spare minute. Spend longer if you can. When you're waiting for something or someone is an ideal time, or on public transport, in a queue, or walking along a corridor at work.

→ Just 'be' in the here and now. Bring your thoughts out of the past or the future into the now. Slow down and feel the moment.

→ Notice people, their expressions, clothing, hair, body language, behaviour.

→ Soak up details of colour, texture and pattern.

→ Really hear the sounds around you: traffic, raindrops, people going about their business, sounds of nature.

→ Feel warmth, cold, the soft breeze on your face, sunshine, the phone in your hand.

→ Really smell the coffee aroma, fragrances or biscuits baking as you pass the shops, or your lunchtime panini or home-made soup.

The surprising power of visualisation

Research confirms that visualisation is another remarkably effective, yet really simple, way to increase confidence and improve how you perform in any situation. All you do is see yourself in your mind's eye going through the situation you want to deal with more confidently. Make this image as clear as you can and, over a few minutes, go through it frame by frame, coping successfully and managing any difficulties that might come up. It may sound a bit bizarre, but it is simple, easy to do and it works.

Dealing with a situation in your mind in advance seems to take the sting out of the nerves and anxiety you feel beforehand, and makes it all very familiar when the day arrives.

Your brain isn't good at distinguishing between what happens in your imagination and the real thing. Think of dreaming. Or imagine now that you're chewing a slice of lemon ... you might find saliva appears in your mouth. So, if you've been visualising a situation, it's as if you've 'been there and done that' many times already, but in a controlled and relaxed way, and these associations then transfer to the real thing for you. Here's what to do.

There are four key things to remember when visualising:

1. You'll be creating a film or video in your mind's eye of the situation in which you want to feel more confident. Make this as clear as you can manage and go through it frame by frame, taking a few minutes (up to 15 or so at most).

2. When visualising, create as much detail as you can: colours, sights, sounds, smells, movement, speech and so on.

3. Before you begin visualising, unwind and relax for at least a couple of minutes. If needed, you'll find ways to do this in every chapter (Chill time). If you feel any stress or anxiety coming on as you visualise, press your mental pause button briefly and use relaxation until the anxiety falls. Then press 'play' and continue with the visualisation.

4. Visualise like this once or twice a day in the days before an event or situation you're not approaching with confidence.

What to do in a visualisation session:

1. Relax your whole body and mind for around two minutes.

2. Now, close your eyes and visualise the event you want to work on, as clearly and in as much detail as you can. See yourself and others, hear what's going on, walk around if it makes it seem more real for you, or speak the words you say out loud.

Hear what is said to you. Experience everything that happens as clearly as you can. See yourself cope with whatever might realistically go wrong on the day. Just the ordinary everyday things, which happen all the time.

3. Spend about 10–15 minutes on this in total.

4. When finished, count yourself back up to normal functioning … 5, 4, 3, 2, 1, fully alert.

In action

Keeping your personal journal

This seems a good place to tell you about another simple way you can use your journal, which will be really useful as you work through the book, and afterwards, when you've finished reading:

➡ As you work through the book, keep three lists on three separate pages, somewhere easy to find in your journal:

1. Changes and techniques you're starting *now*.

2. Changes and techniques you want to start *soon*.

3. Changes and techniques you'll get to *later*.

➡ Including a page reference with each item will make these easier to find later on. You can use these pages to see how you're doing and to remember what comes next.

➡ As time progresses, it's also easy to move items around as they move from *soon* to *now*, or from *later* to *soon* (if you use a reusable 'stickie' for each item, it's even easier).

➡ You can make a start on your three lists by looking back over Chapters 1 and 2.

In short

→ Some common thoughts, assumptions and beliefs (TABs) can be unhelpful in that they limit achievement and lower self-confidence.

→ Becoming aware of these TABs can remove or reduce this effect.

→ Challenging these TABs can also reduce or remove their negative effects.

→ Replacing these TABs with positive versions can improve self-confidence and achievement.

→ Every workplace faces more change and demands than ever before at every level. Every one of the workforce feels the effects of this. But, for some, this is easier to cope with than others, depending on personality, ability to change job, previous experience and existing skill set.

→ Being mindful for at least five minutes a day can boost self-confidence. You can be mindful if you bring your thoughts into the here and now, into the moment, if you slow down and quietly use your senses to take in everything around you and experience the moment fully.

→ If you can visualise yourself calmly and confidently dealing with a situation several times before it happens, this can really improve your performance.

Chapter three

How to say what you really want

What you'll learn in this chapter:	This will help you to be more confident in any work situation, especially:
1. How being more assertive (not aggressive) helps you to say what you really want.	1. Team meetings.
	2. Presentations.
	3. Appraisals.
2. How your body language can be saying more than your words.	4. Managing others/being managed.
	5. Relationships with colleagues at all levels.
3. Different ways to say 'no', without offending people.	6. Your workload.
	7. Bullying or conflict.
4. Ways to cope better with 'put-downs' and conflict situations.	8. Communication at all levels (including letter, e-mail, phone or video) up to board level.

Do you ever come away from a meeting annoyed with yourself because you didn't get your point across the way you wanted? Or perhaps you regret the things you meant to say but didn't? Then there are questions still unanswered and decisions still unmade. If you feel like this more often than you would like, a good way to make a real difference is to be more 'assertive'. And by that I definitely don't mean 'aggressive'. This is a common misconception. Assertiveness is absolutely not about being self-centred or aggressive. Many people still think it is, but it is not so. Assertiveness is about being firm but fair, quietly confident and having respect for yourself and for others. It's about clear and direct communication, and knowing how and when to say 'no'.

How assertive are you at work?

Take a moment to think about assertiveness and you. How much of the time do you feel you succeed in communicating clearly, directly and confidently? Here is a short questionnaire that will assess your level of assertiveness at work.

What to do

Rate whether you agree or disagree with each of these statements and enter your ratings in your journal, in a column, using the scale below. Base your answers on how you are *most days, in typical working situations*. Don't think too long or deeply about your answer. Your first reaction is likely to be the most accurate.

> 1 = completely agree
>
> 3 = agree somewhat
>
> 5 = neither agree nor disagree
>
> 7 = disagree somewhat
>
> 10 = completely disagree

Assess your level of assertiveness at work
1. It can be difficult to speak up and say what I really want to say in meetings.

Assess your level of assertiveness at work
2. I find it hard to refuse requests at work.
3. I find being forceful and uncompromising works well for me.
4. I often let other people have what they want, even though it's not what I want.
5. Giving my opinion in team meetings makes me feel awkward.
6. I say 'I'm sorry' more than I would like.
7. Making others feel guilty is a good way to get what I want.
8. Colleagues take me for granted more than I would like.
9. Instead of asking for what I want directly, I find dropping hints easier.
10. I back down rather than have a disagreement with a colleague.

When you've finished, add up your score. Write this in your journal.

What does your score mean?

1. Check out how assertive you are from this scale:

    86–100   almost always assertive

    61–85   assertive much of the time

    26–60   assertive some of the time

    10–25   hardly ever or never assertive

2. Find out even more about yourself:

    – All of the statements were weighted in the same direction, so those on which you scored 1 show up the areas that you are the least likely to be dealing with assertively.

    – If you've given any statements a score of 10, you are probably behaving assertively in these situations.

So what is assertiveness?

Can you think of a colleague who shouts, pressurises and throws their weight around? And do you know someone who is the opposite: very quiet, rarely draws attention to themselves, does what everyone else wants all the time, apologises a lot and hardly ever expresses an opinion? If you think of these as the two extremes, then 'assertiveness', and an assertive person, will sit halfway between these two.

PASSIVE ◄─────────── ASSERTIVE ───────────► AGGRESSIVE

You can't fail to notice the domineering, noisy, aggressive person and you are likely to be aware of the passive, apologetic person, too. But the assertive person is often less noticeable. They go about their business in a way that gets results, but doesn't draw attention, upset others, or make a fuss. How do they do this? The strength of assertiveness is its core idea that everyone has the same rights and that we should have respect for ourselves and for each other. And it's this attitude, translated into your everyday dealings with colleagues, the public and clients, that has this effect.

Despite having been around for a long time, assertiveness is still often confused with aggression (as I flagged up earlier). But assertiveness is not about being aggressive, stern, severe, harsh, or all the other similar behaviours it can be wrongly mistaken for. What it is about is being able to express your views and needs calmly and effectively and (here is the big difference) in a way that respects both you and the other person involved. So mutual respect is paramount.

What is different about assertiveness is that it's not about special behaviour, or clever words and tactics. What it is about is your attitude, how you see the world and the other people in it. If you can get that right, the rest will follow naturally.

Assertiveness is simply the ability to deal with others in a calm, confident, respectful and effective way, whilst remembering that you have needs and rights, too. The persistence of the confusion between assertiveness and aggression comes about because of a commonly held misconception that the best way to have a view or suggestion heard is to speak loudly and forcefully.

Six key ways to be more assertive at work

Assertiveness is not what you do, it's who you are!

Shakti Gawain, American bestselling author, b. 1948

This chapter will provide constructive suggestions and tips on how you can effect a major impact on your assertiveness through fairly straightforward means. Begin by aiming to be more assertive, more of the time than you are right now, and in the situations you can tackle most easily. You can tackle the more delicate situations, such as that awkward team member, or your line manager, when you feel ready. So what exactly is assertive behaviour? This is sometimes difficult to pin down but, bearing in mind it's based on attitude, here are some pointers.

Six key ways to be more assertive at work:

1. Be aware of your rights as a person and as a member of staff.
2. Know your own needs.
3. Have genuine respect for yourself.
4. Have genuine respect for others.
5. Be clear, open and direct with others.
6. Be able to compromise.

Sounds simple and obvious put like that, doesn't it? But all this can be easy to say, yet more difficult to achieve in the real world. It can be especially difficult if you have past experiences that have given your self-confidence a knock. Here are some examples:

➡ Previous criticism from a manager, colleague, your team, a trainer or teacher.
➡ Overly critical partner, parents or siblings.
➡ Your cultural or social background.
➡ Unpleasant previous experience when expressing your point of view.

Chill time

String puppet

1. Take in a really deep breath, fill your lungs, hold it for a second or two, then let it go with a sigh of relief, dropping your shoulders and allowing all your muscles to relax, just like a puppet whose strings have been cut.
2. Repeat (once only).

Four non-assertive ways people behave

Assertiveness or, to be more precise, the lack of it, has far-reaching effects. It has a major impact on your dealings with the great diversity of people you interact with every day and, in turn, this will have significant consequences for your confidence, identity and self-esteem.

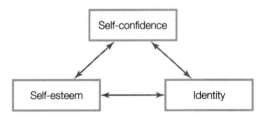

Here are four ways of behaving that are not assertive:

1. **Aggressive**. Angry, rude, noisy, verbally abusive, threatening, domineering, violent, in your face, competitive, using ridicule, dogmatic, insisting on having own way, winning, talking over other people, not listening to colleagues, insisting on being right …

2. **Over-confident or arrogant** (minor aggression). Nothing is a problem, loud, knowing best, full of ideas, interrupting colleagues all the time, knowing everything, one-upmanship, knowing everyone …

3. **Manipulative** (or indirect aggression). Getting your own way by making colleagues feel guilty or by childish behaviour, plotting, sulking, sarcasm or put-downs …

4. **Passive**. Dropping hints, making excuses, being unable to say 'no', the dogsbody, difficulty making decisions, the doormat, a push-over, being unable to say what they want, apologising all the time, putting other colleagues or clients first all the time …

KEY POINT

What does 'passive-aggressive' mean?

People often use the term 'passive-aggressive' in everyday conversation to describe behaviour such as sulking, put-downs or sarcastic behaviour, when this is used to get what you want or to criticise someone. But there is a personality disorder called 'passive-aggressive personality disorder', which can be serious and require treatment, so I feel it's better to stick with the terms 'indirect aggression' or 'manipulative behaviour' when describing that kind of everyday behaviour.

Let's pretend

If you're presenting yourself with confidence, you can pull off pretty much anything.

Katy Perry, American singer-songwriter, b. 1984

So, if you want to be more assertive, where is the best place to start? Change your attitude? Learn how to deal with typical scenarios? Memorise phrases and responses to use? Actually, no. The easiest place to start is with the impression you give with your body and physical behaviour. So, before we go on to think more about attitudes, and about the sort of things assertive people say, let's take time to gain a better understanding of the silent language that speaks volumes about us in the blink of an eye – our body language.

The good thing is, you don't actually have to be confident to look confident. The acting profession pretends to be something they're not every day – and, alright, an Oscar or BAFTA may be beyond your abilities, but just looking confident is not too difficult. You can be like an actor and you can take on the body language of a confident person. You can practise this when no one's about, until you get a feel for it. A couple of practices, like the previous activity, and you're good to go. A bit more practice, and it will almost feel real, not pretend, and you won't even need to think about it. The best of it is, it's a win-win situation. Because if you stand and walk confidently, you will actually feel and be more confident. People will immediately react to you in a more attentive and interested way, reinforcing your confidence, and so on. The next section will tell you how to do this (and there's more about body language in Chapters 4 and 5).

How to walk the walk at work

1. **Aim for an open and relaxed posture**, making good eye contact, and preferably with little or nothing in your hands. Smile if it's appropriate (not too much if you're a woman, as men can mistake this for sexual interest). Open posture means comfortably upright, shoulders back, head up, with no barriers formed by your hands or arms. Arms relaxed by your side or open hands resting easily on your lap when sitting convey quiet relaxed confidence. This overall picture is particularly helpful if you want to have more authority during meetings with colleagues or clients. Any kind of relaxation technique will make this posture easier to achieve, and you'll find one in each chapter. So make sure to practise these, and choose those you like. They really do help.

2. **Make good eye contact**, not too much so it is threatening to others, or too little, which appears nervous and uninterested.

3. **If seated, sit up well and lean forward a little** towards others you might be talking to. This shows interest and encourages people. Slouching back into a chair or a corner can be comforting, but this will appear defensive and aloof or, worse still, apathetic to your colleagues or potential clients, and makes it harder to contribute to a discussion and put your point across.

4. **Don't let your hands give the game away**. Lack of confidence can make you form a fist with your hands or cling to a folder, briefcase or drink, like a comfort blanket. This will be noticed unconsciously or even consciously by those around you. Too many hand or arm gestures also distract and reduce your credibility. If your hands tend to tremble, use relaxation to ease tension – also, imagining your hands being very heavy and comfortably warm is very effective.

5. **Bring down barriers**. Holding one or both arms across your body is a common way of reacting to nerves because you're almost hiding behind them and giving yourself a comforting hug. But this creates a barrier, too, and can be interpreted by your manager or other team members as a lack of interest or, most commonly, as disagreement or disapproval.

6. **Pointing** or staring at someone while you speak appears aggressive and threatening.

7. **Stop fiddling**. Nerves and lack of confidence can make even the best of us fiddle with objects – pens, earrings, coins in your pocket, your hair, your paperwork.

8. **Try making a video-recording** of yourself, or ask a trusted friend or colleague for their take on your body language.

In action

Keep a note of the really useful stuff

1. Go right to the back of your journal and start a new page by writing a heading at the top, 'Useful stuff' (or any other title you prefer).

2. As you work through the book, when you find a particularly helpful idea, thought or explanation, you can make a short note of this, along with the page it was on.

Do you know your rights?

One of the reasons for acting in a submissive or passive way and finding it difficult to assert yourself is not realising that it's not just other people who have rights, but that you have them, too. It's not legal rights or your rights as a member of staff I'm talking about here, just the everyday rights we all have as human beings. Lack of belief in these personal rights grows gradually if you've spent your childhood in circumstances that encourage a lack of belief in your rights. Your workplace environment, past or present, can do the same thing.

Here are some examples. Read them through slowly, one at a time, and make a note of any rights that you're currently finding difficult to apply to yourself.

Your workplace bill of rights

I have the right to:

➡ my own point of view;
➡ have my own values;
➡ be treated as an equal;
➡ ask others to listen to me;
➡ express myself in my own way;
➡ make a mistake;
➡ say 'no';
➡ fail if I try;
➡ try again;
➡ be a leader;
➡ be treated with respect;
➡ ask for what I want.

Always remember:

➡ Each of us has all of these rights.
➡ We deserve these just like everyone else.

Talking the talk at work

Don't let the noise of others' opinions drown out your own inner voice.

Steve Jobs, co-founder of Apple Inc., 1955–2011

With your body language sorted, and an awareness of your rights in place, you're ready to talk the talk. Here are some of the basic assertiveness techniques that will be invaluable in helping you to do that. There is nothing particularly magical or clever about these. Other people use them all the time when communicating with you. Think of colleagues and managers you've found to be fair, respectful and approachable to you. They will be using assertive techniques like these without you even noticing.

Really useful assertiveness techniques	
Respect	The most basic skill of all is to be respectful of yourself and your needs and, equally, of the other person and their needs. This is of fundamental importance in being assertive, and forms the groundwork for all the other skills.
Be short, specific and direct	Always be clear and specific, especially in meetings. Say simply what you are trying to say. Don't start with lots of unnecessary explanation, don't pad things out or waffle. Get to your point and make it clearly.
Ask for information or clarification	This is a good way to make a start to speaking up at meetings, indicate interest or to give yourself time to think. It's also essential for knowing exactly what's being discussed.
Don't be distracted from your point	Don't allow yourself to be 'hooked' by the comments of others, such as 'It's all right for you ...', or 'What about that time you ...'. You'll end up spending precious time arguing over some other fractious or trivial issue, and not addressing the point you were trying to make.

Really useful assertiveness techniques	
Plan and practise first	Don't try to think on your feet, unless it's unavoidable. Work out in advance what it is you want to say, or put across, and where you definitely don't want to go. Think out the actual words you could use. Practise these out loud to get used to hearing the sound of your own voice saying them. Don't over practise, though, or you'll become bored with it and won't sound natural.
Relax	If you tend to feel nervy during meetings, appraisals or other situations, from time to time use one of the quick and easy relaxation techniques found throughout this book, before and during any encounter.
Repetition	A calm repetition of your point or request helps you to stay on track. If the person you're talking to distracts you with excuses or argumentative and manipulative comments, simply return calmly and warmly to your point, and restate it. This is sometimes called the 'broken record' technique: 'I completely take your point, but I really need it by the end of the day.'
Use your voice	Your voice is a huge asset in being assertive. Think about assertive staff you know. What kind of voice do they use? A warm, calm and friendly voice is what to aim for. Lack of confidence or nerves can make your voice high pitched or shrill and carry less conviction. Make a recording and practise, if that helps. (More about this in Chapters 4 and 5.)
Negotiation and reaching a compromise	This is a fundamental skill in assertiveness. After all, you are aiming to acknowledge and respect your needs and those of the other person (or people) involved. Assertiveness isn't about winning at any cost. So, negotiate and reach a workable compromise whenever the situation merits it.

Can't say 'no' to colleagues?

One of the most common difficulties about being assertive is being able to say 'no' to people. And, although there will be many times at work when you can't say no, depending on your job, there will be many occasions, day to day, when you will have a degree of choice. At the very least, there should be the possibility of reaching some kind of compromise, perhaps agreeing on more time for a piece of work. Think of it this way – if you don't say 'no' when you should, you are putting the other person's needs before yours. Is that really your intention? Even in the workplace, there are so many situations when a colleague's needs will be of the same importance as yours and, on some occasions, yours could even be more important. Think about how often colleagues say 'no' to you. You just accept this and don't get annoyed. So why should you worry that they will be upset if you behave the same way?

The real problem is that saying 'yes' all the time can easily become a habit, and changing your behaviour when it's been established like this is really hard. Think about the people around you at work. Do you have a pretty good idea of what to expect from each of them? You probably have. Likewise, colleagues may learn that you tend not to say 'no', so you're likely to attract more requests than you can handle. So, constantly saying 'yes' when you want to say 'no' to requests at work, leads to overload because you'll take on more than you can cope with, or is your fair share. This leads to stress, frustration, ill-feeling, conflict and mistakes and all this entails.

So saying 'no' when you want to is an important skill to crack. This is not about being selfish. There will be times when you decide that you want to say 'yes', even though this might be inconvenient for you. Remember assertiveness means respecting your needs and rights, as well as those of others, and compromising when necessary.

DON'T FORGET

One change at a time

As with everything in this book, take things steadily and don't try everything at once. This is especially true of assertiveness. Try one new skill at a time and practise it till you become fairly good at it. Be ready for the odd setback along the way. You're learning new skills and there are always ups and downs when learning something new.

Different levels of 'no'

Many people find it hard to say no because they think there is just the one way of doing it, the straight 'no'. And this can feel like being rude and aggressive. That isn't usually the kind of impression you want to give in your workplace. You are aiming for good communication, good rapport. But you still have to be able to refuse some requests, to safeguard your own health and well-being. This means being able to say no, but in a way that expresses respect for the other person's needs. But there are different levels of saying no, suited to different situations. Here are the three main options:

1. **A straight 'no'** is the most uncompromising and is rarely suited to the workplace. It is most likely to be used when your rights are being abused in some way. You can add a loud and firm, 'Didn't you hear me, I said "no"', in some cases at work or elsewhere.

2. **Asking for information** or giving a **'rain check no'** opens up a discussion, but still leaves a 'no' of some kind on the table as an option.

3. **A reflective 'no'** is the most sensitive, as you show you've listened to the other person.

I'll explain exactly what these are in the next section, but which one you choose will depend on the situation, how you feel about it and who is doing the asking – it could be a mentor, your line manager, another team member or a colleague you really want to help. But, as mentioned already, don't attempt too many changes in your behaviour all at once – this is especially true for saying 'no', however it is done, because this may come as an unexpected shock to colleagues who don't expect the leopard to suddenly change its spots. Starting small, practising and building up gradually, works best.

Key ways to say 'no'	
Take your time to answer	Give yourself a few moments before you reply to someone's request. Pause slightly or say 'Pardon me?' so they repeat the request, giving you time to think. Or say, 'Now let me think ...', or maybe even check a list or schedule of some sort to give yourself a breathing space to prepare for saying 'no'.
Don't over-apologise	Only apologise if you really want to or it would be appropriate to do so. Many people have a habit of saying 'sorry' far too often! Only use sentences beginning with, 'I'm sorry ...', or 'I'm afraid ...' when it is accurate to do so.
Keep it short	Avoid long rambling explanations of why you can't say 'Yes'. A simple, 'I can't manage it today' will do just as well. These short phrases are also useful, provided they are said with friendliness, warmth and genuine regret: ➡ 'That's a pity, I can't manage it.' ➡ 'What a shame, I just have no time.' ➡ 'Sorry, I can't today.' (Sorry is OK sometimes.)
Reflecting	What you do here is to reflect back the content and feeling of what is being asked of you, but still finish with a refusal. Use a friendly, regretful voice and good eye contact: You: *'I don't have time to help you with the accounts this afternoon.'* Colleague: *'But I really wanted to make a start today.'* You: *'I realise you're keen to get on with it, but I just can't fit it in this afternoon.'* Colleague: *'But, I've got to get it finished this week.'* You: *'I understand that you have to finish it this week, but I just can't help you this afternoon.'*

Key ways to say 'no'	
Broken record	It is important to persist with saying 'no', as people are likely to try to make you change your mind. Children can be particularly good at this! A useful technique for your refusal is 'broken record': simply 'parrot' it back, in a warm voice, no matter what pressure the other person puts upon you.
Reasoned 'no'	This gives, very briefly, the genuine reason for the 'no'. But only give a reason if you want to or need to. You don't have to explain yourself to all the people who make demands on you. ➡ 'I can't help you with your report today because I have a meeting all afternoon.' ➡ 'I haven't got time today because I have to show some visitors round.'
The rain check 'no'	This says 'no' for now, but maybe 'yes' for later. Its name comes from the American practice of giving a 'rain check' to the spectators at a baseball match if rain stops play, which allows them entry to the replay. ➡ 'I can't help you today because I'm in meetings all day, but I might be able to find a bit of time tomorrow.'
Asking for information	This is not a definite 'no', but leaves room for discussion, a compromise, or a later 'no'. ➡ 'How much detail would the report need?' ➡ 'Could you get started on it without me?'
Asking for time to decide	Never be afraid just to ask for some time to think. ➡ 'I need to check my work schedule, then I'll get back to you.' ➡ 'I'm not really sure just now. Can I ring you back later?'

Handling direct criticism

Criticism can be one of the hardest things to cope with in an assertive way. It can hurt your feelings and dent your self-esteem. Sometimes, you can be so fazed by it, that you'll even accept unfair criticism and take it to heart, too. The thing is, there is criticism that is realistic and fair comment and criticism that is unfair and unfounded. And criticism can be made sensitively, and insensitively, in private or in public. You're likely to find yourself at the wrong end of the more upsetting of these at some point in the workplace. That's because not everyone knows how to be assertive, and doesn't always remember to give respect to everyone. And, in some cases, it can be the accepted way of doing things. Let's look at some assertive ways to respond to fair and unfair criticism.

How to react to a criticism that's fair

This can be a difficult one to do but, if you can remember from Chapter 2 that absolutely everyone makes mistakes and that there's always room for improvement, it becomes easier to do. Look out for colleagues doing it. It happens all the time. Here are two ways to handle it.

1. Accept it

The simplest response is to accept the criticism without expressing guilt, giving excuses or making apologies. We all make mistakes and the best thing is to hold your hand up, correct the situation, learn from it and move on. It has been said that the person who never made a mistake never did anything.

Your line manager: *'You didn't make a very good job of that.'*

You: *'No, I didn't did I? I'll have another go at it.'*

2. Ask for information

Another way of coping is to immediately accept the criticism but, in the same breath, go on to ask for more information about it, from the person doing the criticising. Ask a question, any question, about what they've said. It won't matter what you actually ask about, you'll still dilute the criticism and, at the same time, appear confident and still in control.

Your team leader: *'You didn't facilitate that meeting very well.'*

You: *'No, it wasn't too good, was it? Was it the first part, or was it later on that was the problem?'*

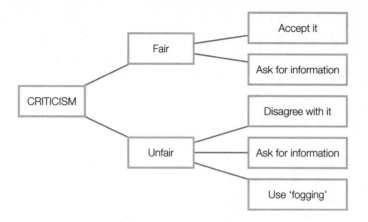

What if a criticism is unfair?

Criticism is often unfair. This happens to us all, and for many different reasons, and it can really hurt even more than a fair criticism. Think back to Chapter 2 and the unhelpful belief that 'Life should be fair' – that's why it hurts more. So, remember that life isn't fair to any of us, but here are three ways to deal with unfair criticism, which may make it hurt a bit less:

1. Disagree with it

Make sure you stay calm and friendly. Think for a few moments, then warmly disagree with the criticism. Here's an example:

Your colleague: *'You're always late for these meetings.'*

You: *'No, I'm not always late … I may have been late once or twice, but I'm definitely not always late.'*

2. Ask for information

You can warmly ask questions and for more information with enthusiasm, until the criticiser wishes he hadn't raised the subject!

3. Use 'fogging'

Fog the issue, making the picture very unclear, by neither agreeing nor disagreeing, giving the criticiser nothing substantial to get a hold on, so that the criticism doesn't hit home. This makes it seem as though the criticism is accepted, but is actually having little impact. This will also put the criticiser off criticising you unfairly again. A bit of practice, and you can become quite skilled at fogging. Including words like *possibly, maybe, perhaps,* or *probably* fogs any issue. Or, try responding with phrases like:

➡ 'Perhaps you are right, these things can happen ...'

➡ 'It's hard to say for sure ...'

➡ 'You could be right ...'

➡ 'There could be some truth in that ...'

What about those subtle 'put-downs'?

Sometimes colleagues, managers or team leaders can be openly critical, and that can be hard enough to cope with. But, now and then, you can find yourself at the receiving end of a 'put-down'. This is a more manipulative and veiled form of criticism. A kind of indirect aggression. Sometimes people don't even realise that they are being insulting and hurtful. You know the kind of thing. Here are some examples:

➡ 'Don't worry, that will do like that. I'll take care of it now.'

➡ 'Are you sure that's the best way to do that?'

➡ 'Haven't you finished that report yet?'

These kinds of comments are usually said in a friendly voice, and maybe even with a bit of a smile, but they leave you with a vague feeling that you've been criticised, but you're not quite sure. A 'smiling assassin', if you like. So you're left not really knowing what to say, and the moment passes. Or maybe you react angrily because you feel instinctively that you're being attacked in some way. But, if you do, the perpetrator just looks bemused and says something like:

➡ 'What? What did I say?'

➡ 'I didn't mean it that way… you're over-reacting.'

➡ 'You're … imagining things … too sensitive … you have an attitude problem.'

Put-downs like these can make you feel small and can undermine your self-confidence. They can become a habit if you let them slip by, and they're difficult to pin down as harassment or bullying. So how do you deal with them?

The foremost tactic is to let the person know in a calm, dispassionate and non-threatening way that you are fully aware of what they've actually implied. Once faced with this reaction, most people will then back down and won't put you down like this again. Colleagues do this to you only if you let them. As ever, practise doing this before trying it for real and only use it if you're sure there will be no unwanted repercussions.

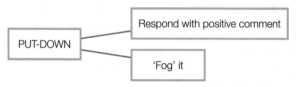

Here are two ways to respond to a put-down:

1. You can acknowledge the criticism, openly, but fairly dispassionately, and follow this up with a positive comment, as in the response to number 1 in the following table.

2. You can reply to an unclear statement with another one – by 'fogging' the issue. So vaguely acknowledge the implied criticism as in numbers 2 and 3. 'Fogging' of this kind can be quite disarming, and disappoints the perpetrator, who then doesn't know if his put-down has hit home or not.

Here are examples of how to respond to the three put-downs mentioned earlier.

	Put-down	Your response
1.	'Don't worry, that will do like that. I'll take care of it now.'	'Yes, you're right. It wasn't up to my usual standard, but I was pushed for time because my planning meeting with my new major client over-ran.'
2.	'Are you sure that's the best way to do that?'	'Yes, I suppose your way of doing it would probably have been better, but Jerry asked me to do it this way today.'
3.	'Haven't you finished that report yet?'	'Yes, maybe it has taken me a bit longer than usual to finish it. But I'm not sure.'

What about criticising others?

You are likely to be involved in giving criticism to others at some point in your career. Most of us exist for the majority of our working life in a sandwich between those who criticise us and those we criticise. Either process can be a source of problems, as both can raise negative and unpleasant feelings if not carried out assertively. Here are some tips:

1. **Praise the positive, too**, on a regular basis. That way criticism will become a lesser part of the feedback you give, and more in proportion. It's common to feel that all you receive is criticism in today's working environment. Give criticism as part of more general and positive feedback, not in isolation, and it will just be a routine event for all concerned.

   – 'You've done a great job. On time, and ticks the boxes. Well done. To make it even better here's a quick suggestion.'

2. **The right to criticise carries responsibilities**. You may be a line manager, with the right to criticise, but this should only ever be used to improve performance, and not for its own sake. Your responsibility is to criticise without being aggressive, attacking or belittling the person. Your responsibility is to criticise assertively, with mutual respect.

3. **Criticise the specific behaviour**, not the person or their personality.

4. **Be considerate** – imagine yourself in the person's shoes. Give criticism in private. Remember, everybody makes mistakes and none of us is perfect.

5. **Keep the big picture in mind**. Be aware of the circumstances surrounding the person, and take this into account. See the situation as a whole, and keep the criticism in proportion.

6. **Criticism shouldn't be a first resort**. Sometimes, just asking someone how the relevant task is going can turn things into a discussion, or even a request for advice or help. This can make criticism unnecessary.

7. **Be sure of your facts** before criticising someone.

8. **Only criticise when you are calm**. If you are angry or upset, wait until you've cooled off before giving criticism.

9. **Don't waffle** and wander round the subject. Come to the point.

10. **Have confidence** in what you are saying. If you aren't sure of yourself or your ground and appear nervy or embarrassed, it makes the whole thing seem bigger and more of an issue to the person being criticised. This rebounds on how you feel and can escalate a minor error into a major catastrophe for you both.

11. **Four typical steps**:

- Your step 1: 'Donna, can we meet this week sometime? I'd like to talk about how your training sessions are going.'
- Your step 2: 'I've noticed that some of the participant evaluations have not been up to your usual high standard – have you noticed this? Why do you think this might be?'
- Your step 3: 'What ideas do you have about making changes to improve things?'
- Your step 4: 'So will we agree that before the next session we can ...'

When disagreement spills over into conflict

In today's world of work and business, there is inevitably going to be conflict, and this is often seen as damaging. There is certainly evidence to support that view, especially if it has gone beyond what you might describe as everyday workplace conflict and has progressed into a situation moving towards grievance and disciplinary action.

But before that level of conflict has been reached, something positive can often come from it, provided it is dealt with carefully. Here are just a few positive outcomes, which can come from conflict, meaning that avoidance it is not always the best strategy:

➡ Increased knowledge and understanding of a situation.

➡ Deeper insight into people.

➡ Stronger mutual respect.

➡ Improved communication and ability to work together.

➡ More knowledgeable about yourself.

There are too many possible scenarios to list here, but the way to approach any conflict is very similar, whether you are involved in it yourself or you have the responsibility of dealing with the situation, and whether two or more people are involved.

Having your say in a conflicting situation

Your aims

→ Reach an agreement, which has not been forced on anyone, approved by all involved, even if this takes more than one session. Focus on solutions, not on problems.

→ The best way to do this is probably the win-win approach: aiming for all sides to leave with their head held high, and with a deeper understanding of the other's position.

→ No matter how difficult it gets, stay objective, and don't get personal.

General guidelines for dealing with conflict

→ **Create some space**. Start by introducing a break and creating enough space for tempers to calm and negative emotions to disperse. During this break, make it possible for those in disagreement to have the opportunity to understand what the problem is. Then clear the way to move forward and resolve things amicably.

→ **Talk about it**. Only when people have reached an awareness of what the problem is, bring those concerned together to talk about it. Think positively from the start, be calm, use positive language and, when needed, the assertiveness skills from earlier in this chapter.

▶

➡ **Ground rules**. The first thing to do at the meeting is to discuss and agree some ground rules such as:

- Everyone treats each other with respect.
- Anyone who becomes angry or aggressive takes time out to calm down.
- Stick to the issue in hand.
- Don't bring up previous history or other issues.
- Keep personalities out of the discussion.
- Separate the problem from the people involved.

➡ **Listen carefully**. Try to look behind the words and behaviour to allow yourself to see the other person's needs and interests – these will help to explain why there is a problem.

➡ **Objective third party**. Sometimes an objective or knowledgeable third party, brought in with everyone's agreement to give information, or act as a neutral arbiter, can shorten the whole process.

➡ **Hear each other out**. Make sure each side listens to what the other side is saying, without interrupting; if necessary, give each a set time to speak without interruptions.

➡ **Break to cool off if needed**. If at any point, things are not working, and tempers are rising again, be prepared to call a halt, and set another time to talk about things when people have had time to cool off.

➡ **Summarise where you are**. When the time seems right, summarise and restate the different points of view.

➡ **Think about solutions**. Now invite both (or more) sides to offer possible solutions and come to some agreement.

In short

➡ Being assertive is a key part of saying what you want to say.

➡ Assertiveness is clear and direct communication coming from a position of respect for the other person as well as for yourself.

➡ Assertiveness lies midway between passive behaviour and aggressive behaviour.

➡ Manipulative behaviour is a form of indirect aggression.

➡ Ways to be more assertive include knowing what you need or want, being able to say this clearly, saying 'no' when you want or need to and being prepared to compromise.

➡ It's best to start small and practise with less important situations.

➡ Skills that are useful include: upright and open posture, steady warm voice, good eye contact, not being distracted from your point, reflection and fogging.

➡ It's usually best to address conflict before it gets out of hand, by letting tempers cool, and then talking things through in an assertive and structured way.

Chapter four

Speaking in front of others

What you'll learn in this chapter:	This will help you to be more confident in any work situation, especially:
1. Ways to be more confident speaking in front of one person, or any group size.	1. Team meetings, or the 'morning huddle'.
2. More ways your body language can improve self-confidence.	2. Presentations.
	3. Giving a talk.
3. Ways to make the best use of your voice.	4. Making a verbal report.
	5. Running training sessions.
4. How to behave more confidently with authority figures.	6. Interviews or appraisals.
	7. Oral tests or exams.
	8. Verbal communication of all kinds and at all levels.
5. How you can be more charismatic.	

Speaking up in groups, large and small, has caused butterflies in human stomachs for thousands of years. Aristotle, the Greek philosopher, wrote three books on the subject in the fourth century BCE. I don't think I've ever met anyone who doesn't have some degree of nerves or anxiety before stepping in front of a group, whether 4 or 400, myself included. Even as an experienced presenter and speaker, I still found that the chattering and expectant sound of an audience waiting in a hall for me to speak produced a stab of anxiety. So, some level of anxiety about speaking in front of others is completely normal, even if your audience is just two or three people, or even just one! I've coached many people who found that training just one other person still produced jitters.

A touch of stage fright?

But if this anxiety or stress seems to be more inhibiting for you than you would expect, there is a lot you can do to feel more confident. Some people naturally feel at ease in front of others, and just adore being in the limelight: TV presenters, famous singers, dancers, actors, and all the rest. But lots of others don't. It's a personality thing. Actress and singer Hayden Panettiere, who is 23, from the US country music drama series, *Nashville*, recently (June 2013) explained in an interview that, when she was just seven, she appeared on Jay Leno's NBC chat show with no nerves at all. But she went on to develop stage fright when she was around 12 and had become more aware of what she was doing. Though much improved, she is still apprehensive before she goes on stage to sing.

But as Chapter 1 explained, if you're not naturally at home speaking in front of others, you'll have other corresponding strengths. In particular, you'll probably be a good listener and organiser and be keen to do well on all tasks, which will more than make up for any shortcomings. Thousands of people feel like a duck out of water when they first try to ski or drive but, with a bit of practice, they soon feel assured and at home.

Others find they are nervous speaking because they've had a bad experience, perhaps the first time they spoke in front of others, and that could have been at home, school or elsewhere. Experiences like that can create a negative association, and avoidance behaviour, as well as doubts about your own abilities – all totally unfounded. Chapters 1, 2 and 3 have explained how to have more faith in your own abilities.

But, even if you're not a natural, or have had bad times, this is a skill like any other, which you can learn all about and practise doing, until you do begin to feel more at home in that situation. One of my colleagues, some years ago, had just graduated and was in her first job. She found herself a complete bag of nerves days before some training she had to do:

> *I knew my subject and was organised and well prepared so, despite myself and my nerves, I did a sound job – not a stunning star performance, but a good solid job. Because I could do the most important parts of the training – being prepared, knowing my stuff and fulfilling the remit. There's no need to have the X-factor, just to do the job and tick the boxes. Star performances and scintillating rhetoric can come later!*

I bumped into her again not long ago and she is now an experienced, able and confident speaker. She still gets apprehensive about bigger groups or if she is addressing her peers or authority figures; but don't we all? After all, nerves in situations like these just show that we care and want to do well, and what's wrong with that? Even the Prime Minister must have nerves on the drive to *Prime Minister's Questions* every week.

Chill time

1-2-3 Breathing

1. Take a gentle breath in to your own slow silent count of 1, 2, 3, then breathe out in your own time, again to your own slow and silent count of 1, 2, 3.

2. Continue gently breathing to this rhythm for a few minutes.

3. With practice, you can leave out the counting and just go into the rhythm when you need to, wherever you are.

Simple changes that can produce large paybacks

Even if you fall on your face, you're still moving forward.

Victor Kiam, American entrepreneur, 1926–2001

The previous chapter focused on assertiveness and introduced the important role of your unspoken body language in being able to say what you want to say. This chapter picks up these ideas and broadens them to encompass speaking and saying what you want to say, while others listen to you. This could be any situation where you are expected to speak on your own, even for a short time, rather than taking part in a social conversation.

This could be contributing to a team discussion, reporting back to the charities committee, training one other person in a specific piece of work, giving a talk to 10 colleagues, or giving a presentation to 200 delegates at a conference. To avoid clumsy text, I'm using *listener* or *listeners* to describe whoever it is you're speaking in front of.

In action

Now, soon or later

➡ As you work your way through this book, start to make up three lists on three separate pages, maybe at the back or centre of your journal.

➡ Here are the three headings as a reminder:

1. Changes and techniques to start on *now*.

2. Changes and techniques you want to start *soon*.

3. Changes and techniques that you'll get to *later*.

➡ And remember, as time progresses, you can move items around as they move from *soon* to *now*, or from *later* to *soon* (if you're using a paper journal, use a reusable 'stickie' for each item, and it's even easier).

Where can speakers go wrong?

This may seem an odd place to start, but it is a sensible one, I assure you. One of the best ways to become more confident speaking in front of others is to address the anxieties you have about it. So, have a think about it – what makes a bad speaker? What is it you don't want to do when you speak in front of others? You're at a meeting at work, and listening intently. What is it that sets your mind wandering off? What annoys you? What makes a poor impression on you? Here are some answers to these questions that I've collected from those around me recently. How many would you agree with?

Speakers can go wrong in the following ways:

- arriving late;
- starting late;
- talking too fast;
- not smiling or introducing themselves;
- giving too much information;
- not pausing to give listeners time to think;
- using content that's not relevant;
- starting a conversation with one person;
- not responding to the listener's reactions;
- spending too long answering questions;
- using lots of gestures;
- telling jokes or stories that are not funny;
- jiggling change or fiddling with their hair;
- not providing necessary notes;
- speaking too slowly;
- not being heard clearly;
- speaking in a monotone;
- patronising the listener;
- criticising people needlessly;
- boring people;
- making it hard to follow points;
- not having any eye contact with listeners;
- talking mainly to the slides;
- using too many slides;
- using too much text on slides;
- taking slides away too quickly;
- using distracting special effects on slides;
- going well over time.

So, you're off to a good start. Just avoid doing anything on this list, and you'll be a good speaker by default. Now, here are some of the more positive skills and characteristics you can easily aim for, to become even better.

Keeping people's attention

What you may not have realised is that, in almost all cases, attention is yours until you lose it. It's a bit like innocent until proved guilty. On most occasions where someone starts to speak, all eyes are on them, and there is an expectant hush. So, all you have to do is keep it that way. You put your head round a door, and everyone turns to hear what you have to say. You're the invited speaker, or you're asked to deliver your report, or you've simply asked a question in a meeting. Everyone will be listening. How you lose that attention is by doing anything on the previous 'bad speaker' list.

Being organised and prepared

1. **Do your homework**. Be as prepared as possible, so that you understand the situation you're going in to, and what your role will be. Whether it's a morning huddle, a quick verbal report to the team meeting, or a formal board meeting, make sure you're up to speed. Ask someone if you have questions. Take the time to have these laid out ready where you want them before you begin.

2. **Plan what to say**. Don't prepare word for word notes to read out. But plan what you'll say, and in what order. Make up short notes and headings to use as prompts and cues. Make sure what you'll need is laid out and easily to hand, and in the right order. Practise if a demo is involved. Get your key statistics, facts and figures together in front of you, along with any names you might forget. Do a run-through before the day.

3. **Try not to do too much**. The commonest mistake beginners make is to try to cram too much into the time available. Think of what *you* would be able to absorb in similar circumstances, and use that as a guide.

4. **Prepare the room**. Make sure what you need will be there, be that flip chart, pens, overhead projector (OHP), DVD player, computer, or whatever. If you are going to use OHP, TV, DVD or computer equipment, arrive in good time to check that they are in working order and to get them set up ready to run.

Ways to make speaking easier

1. **Look at your audience**, scan gently around everyone as you speak to include them. Don't fix your gaze on the back of the room or on one person. Share your gaze with everybody in the room, looking around however many you're talking to with a slow, gentle movement back and forth.

2. **Body language – theirs**. Notice the listeners' body language, and use it to tell you when they are interested in the point you're making, or when you've made your point and they're ready for you to move on.

3. **What to wear?** Something you feel comfortable in, preferably with layers you can shed/add, if necessary. Avoid wearing anything that will distract your listener!

4. **The average human attention span is not long**. After about 10 minutes listening to someone, we are all likely to lose concentration, so it's best to change what you're doing in some way after about 8 to 10 minutes. This is a good time to introduce an anecdote or start some kind of activity or demonstration.

5. **Use your hands** to emphasise and enliven a point, but watch out for over-use and repetitive hand movements which are distracting.

6. **Positioning**. Make sure you are clearly visible and in a central position. Make sure none of the equipment is restricting the listeners' view of you.

7. **Move around** if you can. It is more relaxing and more interesting for you and your listeners, and gives you more authority and presence. But avoid repetitive pacing, like a tiger in a cage!

8. **Mistakes/clumsiness.** Everyone makes mistakes or drops things occasionally, even seasoned presenters. If you appear upset or flustered by this, this can actually make your audience nervous for you, making them feel uncomfortable. The best thing to do is simply acknowledge what you've done, possibly with a quick joke – that helps them to relax and, consequently, you relax too. Quick comments like, 'It's too early in the morning' or 'Needing my lunch', and so on, are useful.

9. **Memory aids**. Bear in mind that people can't absorb or remember every detail of what they hear and they can often lose track of where the speaker is – you do, don't you? So summarise regularly, and have a set of notes to hand out if you want people to take away something more concrete.

10. **Humour** can be very good, too, if used appropriately and confidently. Leave it out if you don't feel sure of yourself with it.

11. **Visual aids, props and anecdotes** all really help to maintain interest, keep it real and get points over (more on this later).

What should you say?

1. **Be prepared.** *Prepare* your content well (see earlier section).

2. **Make it interesting.** Introduce lots of *variety*, and changes of emphasis from what you're saying, to a visual aid to look at, to something for them to do or think about, to a prop to look at, or a well-chosen anecdote, and so on. This maintains their attention and interest and enlivens the whole experience.

3. **Talk to them as equals.** Make it *relevant and meaningful* to your listener. Don't be too theoretical or use jargon, unless you explain what it means and it aids understanding. Avoid talking above or below your group's heads.

4. **Use the 'rule of three'.** The '*rule of three*' technique has been used in writing and in speeches for hundreds of years. It is very powerful and emphasises points, making them more memorable, and more persuasive. So, you might say, 'We can get this project done faster, more cheaply and on time.' Many of today's 'sound bites' use this technique. Here are some examples, old and new:
   - Julius Caesar: *Veni, vidi, vici* (I came, I saw, I conquered).
   - Film title: *The Good, the Bad and the Ugly*.
   - French motto: *Liberté, Égalité, Fraternité*.
   - Tony Blair: *Education, education, education*.
   - Fire safety motto: *Stop, Drop and Roll*.

5. **Make sure they remember.** The old adage for content when public speaking is, 'Say what you're going to say, say it, say what you've said'. This is still a good one, as listeners take in less than you think. Even the adage makes use of the 'rule of three'!

How to get the best from your voice

1. **Getting started**. Speak in clear everyday language. Watch out for speaking too quickly, especially at the beginning, when you might be a little nervous. Make a few very general welcoming statements to start you off, as this lets your listeners tune into your voice. Practise your first few sentences so that you'll be able to remember them, even if nerves kick in.

2. **Pace**. Vary your pace, but never speak too quickly. The pace of everyday speech speeds and slows, so just keep that going. In the first scene of the 2010 film, *The Social Network*, which dramatises the invention and development of Facebook, Mark Zuckerberg is seen speaking to his girlfriend in a quick-fire, non-stop monotone, so much so that she can no longer stand it, and promptly dumps him.

3. **Allowing 'thinking time' for your listener**. We all need this to absorb what's being said. So speak fairly slowly, make points clearly, and leave little gaps for a point to go fully home in your listener's mind.

4. **Tone of voice and mood is important**. Aiming for a warm, gentle, smooth and friendly tone, in tune with what you're saying, is well worthwhile.

5. **Projecting your voice**. For larger groups, a public address (PA) system is likely to be in place and for smaller groups you won't need one. It's the in-betweens that sometimes will not have a PA system. That's alright if you have a strong voice that projects easily. But what if you have a quiet voice that doesn't carry well (as I have) or you are talking to 20 or more people in a hall with poor acoustics and a noisy heating system, or a crèche at the back (as I have!)? Well, you can project even a quiet voice better if you imagine you're speaking to a friend at the other side of the road. Seeing a voice coach can be a great

help, too, if this problem won't go away. You can also bring your own PA system, just like the aerobics instructor or dance teacher. These are easily available, and not too expensive.

6. **Keeping yourself in the mix**. While all of the above are important, keep your own particular brand and style of speaking at the heart of it. Practice helps a lot to blend this all into one complete whole. But never lose sight of who you are.

I'd rather attempt to do something great and fail, than to attempt to do nothing and succeed.

Robert H. Schuller, American motivational speaker, b. 1926

How to get the best from visual aids

Visual aids are any 'aid' used by a speaker in addition to simply speaking – this could be a demonstration of some kind, resources to show to people but, most often, it's a slide show. Though you may think it's more to do with entertainment, the most important use of visual aids is to 'aid' the understanding of the audience by using another medium. This happens in five main ways:

1. It varies the content from speech only.
2. It emphasises the main points of a presentation.
3. It gives structure and order, to help lead the audience through your points.
4. It summarises points once they have been made.
5. It presents figures or graphs.

General tips about using slides

1. **Slide shows**. Computer slide (or acetate) presentations are quick and easy to produce, and very effective. If you are not familiar with the computer software for this (usually Microsoft PowerPoint), sign up for a course. Make sure your slide is being projected onto the screen and is in focus. Take a few minutes to check this out before your audience comes in.

2. **Avoid clutter, bling and small print**. Don't make too many points on a slide. Three or four simple points at most. Nothing too detailed. Use font size 14 or above. Don't be tempted to clutter slides with too much colour, movement and graphics – this actually distracts from your points instead of 'aiding understanding'.

3. **Give people time**. Remember to give time for the audience to take in your slide – they have never seen it before, and need more time than you think to absorb it. Many a group has lost interest in a speaker that way!

4. **Guide your audience**. Summarise where you are often, and regularly point out the part of the slide you are discussing, to keep the audience on track.

5. **Back up**. Always have back-up acetates in case of equipment failure.

6. **Ready for anything!** Be aware of the context you will find yourself in and suit your visual aids to this. You may have hi-tech facilities, or you may just have a white board and pen. Always check what is going to be available. Due to overbooking, I once had to facilitate a training session in a hotel honeymoon suite, with nothing but a flip chart and a few felt tip pens.

Coping with authority figures

Sometimes, people who represent authority can be particularly daunting. Talking to the boss about career progression or salary is a good example of when you might lack confidence. Here are some suggestions, which may make this kind of thing easier to deal with:

➡ Keep in mind the benefits of talking with this person and see it as a stepping stone along the way.

➡ The old ideas like this one still work well – imagine the person or people in authority are in their underwear, sunbathing on the beach, or on the toilet – it helps to make them seem more human and on a more equal footing with you!

➡ Have your questions ready and don't be afraid to have some notes, your laptop or tablet with you – the person in authority will have theirs, so you can too.

➡ Be sure of your facts and know your rights in the situation – do a bit of research first, if necessary.

➡ Keep a 'good' attitude – pleasant, friendly, warm. Keep to your main points – don't be distracted from them. Use the other body language and assertiveness techniques from Chapter 3.

Charisma

In a chapter about speaking to others, it's difficult not to begin to think about charisma. Some people just have this kind of aura or magnetic personality that draws people to them, and encourages people to want to hear what they say, copy what they do, and be more like them. They can light up any room they enter. Princess Diana, Martin Luther King, Beyoncé, Johnny Depp, Nelson Mandela, Marilyn Monroe. Charismatic people communicate and establish rapport effortlessly. So, what exactly is charisma? Pinning down such a nebulous concept is notoriously difficult to achieve.

In action

Rate your charisma

Here are 15 key characteristics of those who are charismatic. Read over them, and rate yourself on a scale of 0 to 10 on each. This will give you a score out of a possible 150. How charismatic are you?

1. Confident but not arrogant.
2. Genuine and respectful of others.
3. Show real interest and liking for other people.
4. An individual who doesn't follow the crowd.
5. Very enthusiastic about your purpose, views and aims.
6. Able to speak clearly and confidently.
7. Able to speak with conviction and enthusiasm.
8. Able to speak with emotion.
9. Not pushy or domineering.
10. Good at 'reading' other people.
11. Good at 'tuning' in with other people.
12. Move with poise and grace.
13. Appear full of energy.
14. Passionate about their beliefs.
15. Calm and confident body language.

Don't be concerned if your score isn't as high as you would like. Few of us are naturally charismatic. But there are ways that you can increase your score on this test, and be more charismatic. Everyone, given self-belief and effort, can develop charisma, either to bring out when needed, or as a more permanent way of being.

Be not afraid of greatness: some are born great, some achieve greatness, and some have greatness thrust upon them.

William Shakespeare, poet and playwright, 1564–1616

Here are ways to improve and develop charisma. There is guidance on how to do all of these in other chapters of this book:

➡ Relax.

➡ Look and sound confident.

➡ Like yourself and like other people.

➡ Be interested in people and sensitive to their needs and emotions.

➡ Be in touch with other people's emotions and your own.

➡ Don't be afraid to show your emotions.

➡ Look and sound positive.

➡ Be self-reliant.

➡ Look and sound full of energy and enthusiasm.

➡ Speak with passion and conviction.

➡ Develop your own vision, purpose and message.

➡ Make people feel special.

IN THE ZONE

Work hard

It's not how smart you are that is the greatest predictor of success on any particular project. Studies confirm that it's how hard you've worked on it. It's the effort you've put in. Think about your past successes and you'll see it's true. So stop putting yourself down for being less able than all your colleagues. Just roll up your sleeves and try harder and you'll make a success of things. And nothing breeds confidence like success.

➡ We all know what we don't like in a speaker, so just avoid all those things, be well prepared and relevant, look confident, and you'll do alright by default.

➡ Vary your pace and tone, take your time and include pauses.

➡ Even for a short report, prepare well and plan what you'll say.

➡ Have a note of people's names you need to remember and other important facts and statistics.

➡ With visual aids, less is more. Don't overdo the special effects on slides, as it's distracting and complicates things.

➡ Slides or overheads are there mainly to provide variety, aid understanding, emphasise and summarise key points, and present diagrams, pictures or graphs.

➡ For small to large groups, scan around your audience as you speak. Don't stare at one person or the back of the room!

➡ Be ready for a power or equipment failure!

➡ You can do a reasonable job in your dealings with authority figures if you prepare well, see it as a means to an end, use your body language and assertiveness skills, and imagine them in beach wear.

➡ Even if we're not naturally charismatic, we can all become more charismatic.

Chapter five

Effortless ways to give the impression you want

What you'll do in this chapter:	This will help you to be more confident in any work situation, especially:
1. Look and sound confident (even when you don't feel it).	1. Team meetings/the 'morning huddle'/video conferencing.
2. Make a good first impression.	2. Presentations/giving a talk.
3. Use eye contact and handshakes to best effect.	3. Running a training session or event.
4. Change an unsatifactory first impression for the better.	4. Interviews.
	5. Meeting new people, e.g. clients, colleagues you haven't met, new business partners.
	6. Communication at all levels (including letter, e-mail and phone) up to Board level.

Ancient meets modern

This chapter will explain more about how simple changes to body language can make you appear more confident when it counts. That all-important first impression really does matter. From a run-of-the-mill day at work, to a training day off-site, or that vital presentation or interview, or even asking for a raise. But, if you want to give the desired impression, not just at first, but always, you need an understanding of how our ancient body language heritage still has power over our every move.

This important subject was introduced in Chapter 3, when we looked at saying what you really want. We also started you off on how to 'walk the walk and talk the talk'. In this chapter you'll learn more quick and easy ways to look and sound confident, even if you don't feel it. You'll discover how simple changes in posture, eye contact, facial expressions, handshakes and greetings can transform the impression you're giving, and give you a fantastic start in appearing confident. And when you look confident, not only do you feel more confident, but you'll find that others react to you accordingly, and that adds still more to your confidence, and so on. Win, win!

Why body language matters

But I'm not a sad, depressed, miserable person. I guess sometimes I give off that impression.

Edward Furlong, American actor, b. 1977

There are various estimates, but most experts reckon that, when we meet someone new, we form something like 90 per cent of our impression of them within the first 60–90 seconds of seeing them. This is a skill all humans have. We don't even need to think about it. It just happens. Even your first few sentences, as articulate and well thought out as they may or may not be, are likely to be overlooked in favour of the impression you are giving through how you are sounding, your accent, choice of words, what sort of greeting you've used, how much eye contact you make, and what you are wearing.

That's one of the reasons it's so hard to remember people's names when we are first introduced to them, especially if there are two or three new people, or more. Our processing systems are too busy taking in how people look and sound, and what that might mean, and how we might appear to them, rather than establishing a clear memory of their names.

When you next meet with friends or colleagues, when you are introduced to a new person at work, or you're standing in the supermarket queue, notice how you are forming impressions of people around you, without really being conscious of it. It's something we all do. And we all do it far better than you might think. We're all really good at it. We do this without thinking, usually oblivious to how other people's body language is affecting us. We are just aware of the conclusions we are drawing from it.

So, you might feel you can't trust a colleague, but can't quite explain why. Or you can take an instant liking to a new team member, after a 10-minute meeting. This rather swift and superficial behaviour evolved in primitive times, with the main function of keeping us safe. Being a quick and accurate judge of people was an immensely important skill to have, before society formed with all its unwritten rules and police back-up. You never knew whether an approaching stranger, or friend for that matter, would attack you, or steal from you. So you had to be a good judge, and a quick one, for your own safety.

In action

Silent language

You'll need your journal, a clock, watch or timer to time two minutes, and access to a two- to three-minute recording that you haven't seen before and can play back – this should contain everyday interactions you haven't seen. You could use one of these:

➡ DVD player and a drama DVD (rating 15 or below and not horror or science fiction!).

➡ TV playback facility, such as BBC iPlayer, or any website with videocasts.

➡ TV with automatic replay, or TV and digital recorder.

1. Whichever equipment you're using, have your recording ready, and keep the sound turned off to begin with; make sure you can play back about two to three minutes of the recording.

2. Now choose a recorded section that will last for at least two minutes, and with at least two people on screen, that you've never seen before, interacting in a fairly normal, social way – a chat show, drama, soap, documentary, someone talking to camera, and so on.

3. Now, keeping the sound off for two minutes, focus on one person on screen you've never seen before, and use your journal to make a note of your silent impression of that person:

   – approximate age;

   – what job they do;

   – what their personality is;

   – what they sound like;

   – anything else you want to note.

4. How detailed an impression did you get of the person in a silent two minutes?

5. Did you like or dislike the person from your silent impressions?

6. Now watch the same two-minute section again, this time with the sound on. Note down anything else you can now add to your impression.

7. How does your impression with the sound off compare to the one with sound on? What did hearing the person talk add to your impression? Has any part of your impression changed? Did the person's voice or accent change your impression?

For most people, their impression with the sound on will not change greatly (unless the person's voice is very different from what was expected). There are two reasons for this:

1. First impressions are hard to change.

2. Although this varies in different situations, most of the impression you have of someone comes from their body language and not the actual words they say.

I've no idea what they make of me. People don't usually recognise themselves in an impression.

Rory Bremner, Scottish comedian and impressionist, b. 1961

How to change a first impression

We all know that first impressions can be terribly wrong. Almost everyone has had first-hand experience of this, by giving a first impression we regret. And this is very difficult to change. The best way to 'undo' a bad first impression is to create a better one in a range of other contexts. This helps to dilute the effect of a bad first impression much more effectively than making a huge effort wherever you were originally – work being a typical example. So, go to the team-building course, volunteer to collect for charity or abseil off a tall crane, attend hen or stag nights, and go along to the Christmas party. But take care to make the impression you want in all these other places, and ensure that those you want to impress will see you there. Showing photographs or putting them up on Facebook or other social media sites may well be quite effective, too. This has certainly changed my impression of quite a few people I know. An acquaintance I had always thought was quiet, with little to say, revealed herself to be witty and interesting when I read her popular posts on Facebook, which never failed to attract lots of attention.

DON'T FORGET

Even if you feel you've planned and prepared, and said all the right things, your body language may be letting you down. The silent and subconscious signals that your body is giving can be communicating something quite different from what you are saying verbally. But you can put that right!

Staying out of the loop

So, if lack of assertiveness and low self-confidence show through your body language before you've said a word, it's well worth doing something about it. This gets you off to a bad start whenever you meet someone, or when you come into a room. It's then a bit of a vicious circle. People react to your passive body language, you notice this, making you feel even less confident, which shows in your body language, and so on. But it's really easy to do something about that. Changing body language is much easier to do than changing the words you use.

In the picture

Find a time and place when you can be on your own for half an hour or so. You'll need your journal and a video recorder, camera, mobile phone or other device that can record for at least a minute or so (or just use a full-length mirror).

1. Stand facing the recording device, adjusting this so you can see full length. Make a trial recording to check everything's working, and to get used to the idea. Make a few short recordings, if needed, to lose your self-consciousness.

2. For the following actions, make a recording (or just watch yourself in the mirror). Try again if it doesn't work first time:

   - Recording 1: For about 30 seconds, stand as if you were talking to someone. Look at the recording lens (or mirror) as you would look at the other person. Say a few words if that seems more natural. Or just mime them.
   - Recording 2: Now move away and walk past the lens (mirror) in your everyday walking style, first from one side, then from the other.

3. Play back the two recordings, one after the other, thinking about these questions. Note down your thoughts in your journal if you want to:

   - Recording 1: How were you standing? What did you notice about yourself? What impression are you giving? Be honest! What improvements would you make?
   - Recording 2: How did you walk past? Anything particularly noticeable? What kind of impression are you giving? How could you make improvements?

4. How do you come into a room? Reposition your camera (or mirror), if necessary, to record yourself coming through a doorway: ▶

- Recording 1: Take a moment or two to imagine you're going to be coming through a closed door to join a meeting at work. There are already five or six people in the room, round a table. You know the facilitator, but not all of the others. Imagine this really clearly, and feel the way you would be feeling. Now, press record, go out of the room, close the door, then come back into the room, the way you would in the situation you've been imagining. Have a trial run first if you want, without recording.

5. Play back the recording and describe yourself under these headings:

   a) How fast you moved, and your overall body posture (upright, stooped, relaxed, tense, etc.).

   b) Does your head come in first, then your body? Do you come half way in then hold back a little?

   c) How far did you open the door? How do you hold your head?

   d) Where were your arms and what were they doing (e.g. by your sides, in pockets, holding onto something for comfort)? Shoulders (relaxed, hunched up, tense)?

   e) What about eye contact when you came into the room? Where were you looking?

   f) How and where would you sit? Slowly find a seat, sit down as quickly as you can, first possible seat, a corner, near the door, away from or near the facilitator?

   g) What overall impression have you given to the people in the room, who've never met you before?

6. Now think about confident people – using the same headings as in Question 5, note down how you think they would come into a room, in the same situation.

7. Now try coming into a room again, this time in the confident way you've described in Question 6. Record this if you want to.

8. How did this feel? Could you see a difference?

Handshakes

When you meet someone new, the first thing that often happens is a handshake. You may not think much about this, but the wrong kind of handshake can give a compelling impression and, if it's not the impression you wanted to give, that impression can be hard to shift. But I'm not referring to any kind of group handshake. That's outside the scope of this book.

Have you ever been given what is known as the 'dead fish' or 'cold fish' handshake? This is what it sounds like, cold and limp, sometimes a little damp, and hardly gripping or engaging with the other person's hand at all. It feels unpleasant, and most people relate it to the person giving it having a weak character, or not showing respect. Those giving this kind of handshake are usually totally unaware that they are doing it.

The confident way to shake hands is to reach out your hand strongly and decisively towards the other person, your thumb pointing upwards, and your fingers all pointing straight towards the other person. You're offering them your hand in a relaxed and comfortable gesture of friendliness and openness, using a movement that has developed over many years to demonstrate trust and welcome. When the other's hand is offered, grasp it fairly firmly, but not so firmly as to be uncomfortable, then pump up and down two or three times, with a warm smile and good eye contact. Then, unhurriedly, break contact.

What to wear

O would some power the gift to give us to see ourselves as others see us.

Robert Burns, Scottish poet, 1759–1796

Have a look in the mirror or at recent photos or videos of yourself. Try to take a mental step backwards and look dispassionately at what you see. Look around at other professional people of a similar age and background. How are they looking? What are they wearing? Years can pass and we are still wearing the same style of clothes and the same hairstyle. Not deliberately, but just because they suited you, you liked them, or life was just too busy to even think about it. Are there any changes you would like to make? Weight, style, fitness, hair, clothes, whatever? Women are taken more seriously in clothes that don't draw attention to their femininity. So, go for trousers or a skirt length on the knee or below, and choose lower heels and pale or pastel-coloured lipstick. A new, healthy, fit and more modern look and, if necessary,

losing or gaining a few pounds, too, can make a huge difference to your confidence and self-esteem.

Chill time for the mind

Imagine

To relax your mind, first relax your body as much as possible (use
any of the book's relaxation techniques). Then, for one to three
minutes, picture in your mind's eye as clearly, and in as much
detail as you can, a calming scene such as:

➡ waves lapping on the seashore;

➡ boats bobbing in the harbour;

➡ dark, deep, green velvet;

➡ another image you find relaxing.

Eye contact

Feeling unsure of yourself has the effect of reducing your eye
contact with other people. This makes others feel uncomfortable, and not quite sure what to make of you. It's said that the
eyes are the window to the soul, and that may be so, but the
eyes are definitely how we really get to know someone, and
make judgements about what makes them tick, how moti-
vated and enthusiastic they are, and even whether we feel as
they do or trust them.

Making good eye contact is clearly very important to the
impression we make. So what should you do? What is 'good
eye contact'?

➡ If you make eye contact for around *two-thirds of the time* that's
  usually about right for a social or workplace conversation.
  Women tend to use eye contact a little more than men do.

- Keeping eye contact for *too long can seem disconcerting* or negative. Similarly, if you look away too much, this can make you seem uninterested, or distracted.

- So, on a first meeting with someone, as a very rough guide, look for three to four seconds, then glance away for one to two seconds, then look back for another three to four seconds, and so on. It's probably better to *look more when you're the listener*, and look away more when you're talking.

- When you *break eye contact*, do this in a slight downward direction, as this shows interest. Breaking contact upwards, or to the side, gives different impressions and looks odd. Try this out on a friend or in the mirror, and see!

- If there is a *height difference*, it's always better to try to sit down somewhere, so that your eye level becomes closer to the other person. Or stand if others are seated. If you are a woman who would prefer to be taller, it can help to wear heels to compensate, but not so high that walking becomes awkward and defeats the purpose. Confident people are always perceived as being taller than they are, so just act and talk tall!

Your headlines

Aim to have your head upright and directly facing someone you're talking to or, better still, slightly tilted to one side, as this shows interest and support for what's being said. Tilting your head downwards slightly, but with eye contact can appear disapproving or dismissive. Tilted further down with little eye contact appears passive and withdrawn and is very off-putting to others. But nodding at appropriate moments and using facial expressions and eye contact, which reflect interest and understanding, are all good.

Joining the magic circle

With standing or walking meetings and 'morning huddles' becoming more common, you can find yourself standing in a group at work. If you're having a conversation with one other person, don't stand straight on to them, as this can seem overbearing. Standing at about a 90 degree angle (or right angle) to the other person is about right. Three people will usually stand in an equal-sided triangle, four in a square, and so on. We mostly do this entirely without thinking, and a group will open up and extend the shape to a pentagon, then a hexagon, as more people join the group. Have a look at people standing talking in the street or in a shop or night club, and you'll see this in action. A group of women dancing in a circle is the natural progression of this.

Cultural differences

All that has been covered so far about body language applies to interactions involving people from the same cultural background in a western or industrialised-type society. When people from the same cultural or ethnic background interact with one another, they can very easily read the other's body language, as they share that language. But each cultural background has its own specific body language. Even a simple gesture can have a quite different meaning.

So, if both you and the other person are from the same non-western background, your own particular set of rules will apply. But, if you have a meeting with someone from a different cultural background from your own, there will be differences, and these can be significant. So, best to check this out in advance. Even what you may believe to be universal may not be. Crucially, in business, a head shake or nod does not always indicate 'no' and 'yes'. If there's no time to explore these variations, observe their body language closely, especially eye contact, body space and handshakes, and try to reproduce these.

Take it slowly

If some of what you've been reading makes some kind of sense to you, don't try to take too much on board all at once. Work on changing one thing at a time. You can always refer back to this book for more ideas, once you've mastered a few main changes. Which will these be? Where would you start? Make a note of these in your personal journal under *now, soon* and *later.*

Man needs his difficulties because they are necessary to enjoy success.

Abdul Kalam, former President of India, b. 1931

In short

→ Getting your body language right will instantly make you look more confident and feel more confident.

→ We form almost all of our impressions of new people we meet within the first minute of meeting them, and from how they look and sound, rather than what they say.

→ First impressions are hard to change, but it can be done.

→ You can speak a thousand words, just in the way you come into a room and sit down.

→ Avoid using a 'dead fish' or 'cold fish' handshake. A firm but comfortable grasp conveys a much better impression in that crucial first minute.

→ Eye contact speaks volumes, and should be about two-thirds of the time.

→ Maintain a smart, up-to-date business appearance.

→ Take time to make any changes, and do this one change at a time. Use your personal journal to keep things moving along.

→ Before making any changes at work, do try this at home!

Chapter six

Getting on with other people

What you'll learn in this chapter:	This will help you to be more confident in any work situation, especially:
1. The benefits of listening to other people 'actively'. 2. Fast and effective ways to build rapport with others. 3. Ways to get on well with the others in your team. 4. What you can do to make managing and being managed a better experience.	1. Team meetings/the 'morning huddle'/training sessions/ other meetings. 2. Networking of all kinds. 3. Managing and being managed. 4. Work-related social events. 5. Work-related team-building events. 6. When small talk is needed. 7. Communication at all levels, including by letter, e-mail and telephone, up to Board level.

Not that long ago, it would have been relatively easy to name all the jobs people could be doing: plumber, electrician, engineer, doctor, nurse, teacher, and so on. Doing this today would be impossible, such is the range and variety of occupations. And almost all involve interacting with people some or all of the time, whether that is colleagues, clients or members of the public. So, getting on with other people is something almost all of us have to do every day. This chapter will home in on this fundamental part of your daily work experience, and brush up on your skills and techniques so that you can improve, and even transform that experience, and so give your confidence in such everyday matters a boost. All of the book's earlier chapters will already have had something to add to this, too.

Talking to people

This most basic of workplace abilities is one that may pass us by when we think about the key skills that can define how well we personally perform, and how our organisation performs. And yet, if you think about it, with all the varied work-based activities we take part in every day, how we talk to people has to be one of the most pivotal. So, having more self-confidence in this most commonplace of behaviours can only produce tremendous benefits for you and your company.

Most of the time in the workplace, everyday social conversation is not appropriate, and we use other ways of communicating, almost without thinking about it in our many different interactions with people every day, from brief small talk with a new colleague, to regular team meetings, talking to your manager or staff, taking part in an appraisal or a Board meeting, talking with HR or Occupational Health, and so on. Each of these will involve one or more quite distinct ways of communicating. And, when several different communication styles are needed, they usually have to come in the right order, too. Most of your dealings with people will begin with small talk.

The following table shows other common ways we communicate and when they can be used. In this chapter, you'll find different ways of improving your technique in each.

Common ways to communicate	Used in situations like these
Small talk	➡ Meeting a colleague for the first time. ➡ Before a meeting or a course begins. ➡ On arrival at work. ➡ The beginning of a business call. ➡ With clients. ➡ Networking. ➡ Interviews. ➡ With those you don't know well at lunch or coffee breaks, travelling or work-based social events.
Social conversation	➡ Lunch or coffee break with colleagues you know well. ➡ Work-based social events with colleagues you know well. ➡ Travelling together with colleagues you know well. ➡ Networking.
Supportive exchange	➡ Team meeting. ➡ Talking to a colleague with a problem. ➡ Managing others or being managed. ➡ Appraisal. ➡ Human Resources interaction. ➡ Occupational health interaction. ➡ Employee assistance interactions.

Don't blow hot and cold

We all know people who are different each time we meet them: friendly today, stand-offish tomorrow. It is difficult to develop and maintain a good relationship in such circumstances. If this is your manager, a client, or a team member you work with much of the time, this can make the daily grind even harder. We never really know where we are.

➡ If this inconsistent behaviour is you, become aware of it and how difficult it makes working with you. Being the same this morning as this afternoon, and the next time you meet someone, and the next, is a very positive characteristic and something for you to aim for.

➡ If it's a colleague, you may be blaming yourself, and looking for reasons in yourself for his chameleon-like change of behaviour. So, know that it isn't you who is causing it. It's just a personality thing, or perhaps is brought about by something that's happening in your colleague's personal life or their working life behind the scenes. Your best approach is to remain consistent and friendly yourself, and use active listening, assertiveness and other skills in this and other chapters to make sure that his behaviour does not have a negative effect on you.

Closed questions close down a relationship

In all kinds of communication, using too many closed questions will put the brakes on it. A closed question is one that can be answered with a 'yes' or ' no', or very few words. These create a very one-sided conversation and are particularly poor for developing rapport. Time pressure and habit can mean that colleagues, team members or line managers can slip into this kind of staccato conversation with their staff often without realising it. Here are some examples:

✗ 'Did you have a team meeting yesterday?'

✗ 'What's your new client's name and phone number?'

✗ 'When is the Chief Executive's visit?'

So, choose your questions with a bit of thought. Aim to use open questions or statements, which take a few sentences or more to answer, and create a more balanced, interesting and supportive discussion. Here are examples of alternative ways to ask the above three questions:

✓ 'How was your team meeting yesterday?'

✓ 'Tell me about your new client.'

✓ 'How do you feel about the visit from the Chief Executive?'

This will add depth to the conversation, and allows rhythm and rapport to develop easily. Open questions or statements will usually begin with words such as:

✓ how

✓ tell me about

✓ what did you think of …

✓ describe

✓ in what way

✓ what about

✓ how do you feel about …

How to do small talk

You may find the idea of 'small talk' boring and time-wasting. Many people do but, unfortunately, socialising of all kinds usually opens with small talk and it definitely forms the bedrock of good rapport and long-lasting relationships, both in and out of the workplace. Most of us could benefit from brushing up on our small talk. I seem to be stuck in a rut with the weather as my usual topic. But, then, I live in the west of Scotland, where we can have four seasons in one afternoon!

1. **For people you already know**, small talk usually begins with your version of, 'How are you?', then moves on to everyday topics of common interest like the weather, the traffic or big news stories, then moves on to more personal areas, such as asking about partner, family or job.

2. **On a first meeting**, you're more likely to begin with introductions, then move to comments about where you are and why. Perhaps at a training day or a team-building afternoon. Conversation then moves on to general discussion of where you're from or your job. People like to get a thumbnail sketch of someone before moving forward with small talk. There would be no point in asking someone who is facing possible redundancy where they are going on holiday that summer, or complaining about having to take time out of your schedule to attend a course, if you're speaking to the tutor.

3. **Keep a bit of an eye on the news** and current affairs, even if you don't usually and you have no interest. It's definitely worth the effort. Think of it as a means to an end. Buy a popular newspaper or magazine regularly to keep up with 'what's hot and what's not', or just skip round popular websites and TV programmes every so often. It's not detail that matters, just an idea of what's being talked about, or 'trending' on the internet and socially. This will never go wrong and will reap benefits in building stronger relationships, both new and old.

Social conversation

Imagine if two people are talking, and the person who is speaking holds a large red ball, then passes it to the other person when they speak. If you think about it, in most everyday social conversations, each person would have the ball for about an equal amount of the time. The ball would pass back and forth, with the rhythm of the conversation, a bit like a regular and long-lasting tennis rally.

Here are two participants in a one-day training course, Adele and Luka, having an everyday conversation over lunch. They know each other slightly and work in different companies. They begin with small talk, then move into social conversation:

Luka: *How are you today?*

Joanne: *I'm good thanks, what about you?*

Luka: *Yes, doing OK, thanks. Seems a good course.*

Joanne: *It's been a useful morning, yes. The trainer puts it over well.*

Luka: *I've waited months to get on this course. Just couldn't get the time.*

Joanne: *How's Caroline? Still with Kerr and Simpson?*

Luka: *Just had a step up, yes. They're doing well. How's baby Danielle? Still got that cute smile?*

Joanne: *Yes, she's a sweetie. Her dad's looking after her while I'm away.*

Luka: *We're just back from two weeks in Italy. Had a great break. You getting away soon?*

Joanne: *Next month. Heading for the snow. Just love skiing. Do you ski?*

Everyday social conversation has this kind of back and forth rhythm, with 'turns' being taken in a roughly even and equal pattern. Each person takes their turn and will ask a question, offer some feedback, or reflect back, then pause slightly, looking at the other person, indicating it's their turn to speak. We all do this completely without thinking, having learned to do this from our parents' 'baby talk' during infancy.

DON'T FORGET

In social conversation, aim for a balanced conversation, with each person speaking for roughly the same time. If one person dominates the conversation, this is experienced as boring or self-centred by the other. We've all felt the bitter taste of the person we bump into when we ask, 'How are you?', and they then give us all their complaints, then head off without asking how we are at all.

Supportive exchange – active listening

Listening in this kind of situation is probably more important than talking. Although listening in such situations is not the passive experience you might think. If someone were to just sit and listen to us, nothing more, it would soon feel very strange, and you would wonder if they were really listening at all. That's because good supportive listening is really an active process, much more active than social conversation. The listener says less than the speaker, yes. But what an active listener is doing is hearing what is said and understanding it, and then showing this through a few careful words, or a nod of the head, and a quiet, 'Go on'. So, good listening is not as one-sided as you might expect. And though you're overtly saying and doing less, your mind is more active and analytical than in social conversation.

There are many simple ways you can listen more supportively, just by listening more actively. Here are 10 very straightforward ways to do this:

1. Really listen, and pay attention.
2. Engage mentally with what is being said.
3. Be interested – people can be fascinating if you let the barriers fall, and just let it happen.
4. Pleasantly warm, light, surroundings, with a minimum of clutter, and preferably no barriers such as a desk between you instantly shows you are taking the conversation seriously.
5. Give the person the courtesy and respect of not being interrupted by phone calls, text messages or people dropping in.
6. There's no need to think of smart solutions and clever things to say, and you don't have to move into a role that is more like counselling or coaching.

7. Hear the emotion in the words and the voice, be alert to body language, and reflect on what may lie behind these. Observe feelings.

8. At appropriate times, nod, or say 'uh-huh', reflect or summarise what's been covered, ask a question or for more information.

9. React appropriately to what's being said. No smart answers or response needed – just reflect back what you've seen or heard, and the other person will feel heard and continue to explain. For example, you could say:
   - 'I can see how angry this has made you feel.'
   - 'What Kate did has clearly increased your workload considerably.'

10. If someone has just told you about an experience or a piece of work in which they have shown a strength of some kind, comment on that strength:
    - 'Your report was so well organised and easy to read.'
    - 'You showed such initiative there.'

Supportive exchange – empathy

Empathy is probably one of the most underrated of abilities. It's a key part of being able to listen actively, and in any kind of supportive exchange. It can also open the door to building a good rapport. Empathy is simply the ability to feel what it's like to be in another person's shoes, or to put yourself in their position. It's something that comes quite naturally to many people. But, if you're not one of them, it can be learned, too, as it is the fast-acting glue that can form strong relationships very quickly. If you've never thought about empathy before, it can just be a case of becoming aware of it, and all sorts of improvements in your working relationships (and personal ones, too) can follow.

Empathy is the ability to have a deep understanding of another person's world, and you can show this by:

→ Putting yourself mentally in their shoes to find out what it feels like.

→ Using a warm tone of voice.

→ Using good eye contact.

→ Reflecting back what a person is saying to you, e.g. 'I can see your meeting with the client was disappointing for you.'

→ Provided you practise this first so that it's not obvious – try breathing in unison with the other person, and speaking at the same pace.

But watch out for being tempted to say anything along the lines of, 'I know how you feel', to show empathy because it is invariably met with the response of, 'Nobody knows how I feel' or 'No you don't'. People frequently feel that they are experiencing something that no one else can understand, unless they've experienced it, too. You've probably felt like that yourself at some point. Empathy is usually better expressed by words such as:

→ 'I can't begin to understand how awful you must be feeling today …'

→ 'I can only imagine what that must feel like for you …'

Being able to speak with warmth is another key part of supportive exchanges and is also important for good communication, assertiveness and good rapport, too. We all know people we would regard as 'cold', so we all know intuitively what 'warmth' is, and we certainly can recognise when it is absent. But it's a difficult idea to explain or define exactly. You can show warmth:

- through empathy;
- your tone of voice;
- speech rhythm;
- open and relaxed posture;
- smiling appropriately;
- using good eye contact.

Just take a look at a mother talking to her baby for a clear demonstration of all of these. Even fathers feel more at ease these days talking to their young children in this way. If you have a child or a well-loved pet, compare your tone of voice and speech rhythm when they've just run across the floor with muddy feet, with when you're having a bit of a cuddle. Warmth, like empathy, is difficult to fake. It has to be real and come from within you. The famous American psychologist Carl Rogers (1902–87), founder of this kind of approach, thought of warmth as 'unconditional positive regard', in other words, 'I am positive towards you, no matter what'.

DON'T FORGET

Active listening

This can be so much more interesting and engaging for you, than just passively listening. This also means it will be much easier to remember what has been said to you and will give you other benefits, too. People feel valued and important if you remember what they've said to you, and this is great for building a strong relationship. Who do you know who always remembers your name? Or never forgets what you told them last time you saw them? How did that make you feel? This brings us to the topic of remembering and to memory.

How rapport can work for you

The word 'rapport' comes from the French word *rapporter*, which means to return or bring back. This also brings to mind the commonly made comparison that a good conversation is like a game of tennis. The 'service' ball, or opening remark, is returned by the other player, and then there is a good volley, with the ball going back and forth, just as a good conversation does, with each player enthusiastically having their turn.

You'll know what it's like when you have a good rapport with someone. It's easy and comfortable, and you feel you are being heard and taken seriously. There is a sense of being really understood. You are encouraged because the other person is interested in what you are saying, and they respond to you in an appropriate and meaningful way which takes the conversation along at a favourable pace, in a useful direction. So, building a rapport is about having a productive two-way conversation, which has a rhythm, enthusiasm and momentum of its own. So it's about high-quality two-way communication.

DON'T FORGET

Most of our communication is done through tone of voice, facial expression and body language. Estimates vary, but less than 10 per cent of communication is done through the actual words we use.

Simple ways you can build rapport

So, whatever the interaction, a good rapport is a valuable starting point and a sound basis to work from. Think about those people you're pleased to bump into, have a meeting with at work, or are happy to hear at the end of the phone.

What is it about them that means you enjoy meeting and talking with them?

Then there are the people you find it hard to communicate with, difficult to connect with, or get through to. What is it they are doing that puts you off? What is it about some people that makes your heart sink a little when you have to talk with them? This may seem a back to front approach, but one of the simplest ways to build rapport is to make sure that you *don't* do certain things, just like being a good speaker in Chapter 4. If you simply avoid certain behaviours and characteristics, you'll have made giant steps towards establishing a rapport already.

The more you talk to people and become interested in them, the more they'll give back to you, and you'll find that even the most apparently insignificant, quiet and mousy looking person has a story to tell, and sometimes a more fascinating one than you could ever imagine. Appearances and first impressions can be very misleading. So, making people feel good about themselves and feel important is really easy to do in a genuine way. And from this comes good rapport. Just listen, and ask questions that follow on from what they've said:

➡ 'How interesting, tell me more.'
➡ 'What a surprise – how did you manage that?'
➡ 'Well done, you! Tell me all about it.'

Here is a non-exhaustive list of do's and don'ts for quickly and easily creating a strong and long-lasting rapport. Are some of your own thoughts included?

Aim for these to promote rapport ✓	Avoid these to promote rapport ✗
Open mind	Talking too much
Unconditional acceptance of others	Talking for too long without thinking about the commitments of others
Respect for others	Taking phone calls or texts during your conversation
Empathy and warmth	
Liking for others	Giving friendly pushes or back slaps
Commitment	
Positive comment on strengths	Dominating the conversation
Good listener	Dominating or manipulating them
Patience	Pushing your own views on them
Honesty	Judging them
Use of the person's name	Not responding to what they're saying
Consistency	
Understanding	Complaining endlessly about your own problems
Interest in people	
Positivity	Not asking anything about them
Sense of humour	Interrupting them
Talk about common interests	One-upmanship
Cheerfulness	
Genuineness	
Trustworthy	
Remembering previous discussions	

Before you speak ask yourself if what you're going to say is true, is kind, is necessary, is helpful. If the answer is no, maybe what you are about to say should be left unsaid.

Bernard Meltzer, American radio host, 1916–1998

Are you emotionally intelligent?

There are numerous physical and practical capabilities that are essential for the work we do, be that as an architect, lawyer, teacher, doctor, sculptor, nurse practitioner, or whatever. Physical attributes, such as a steady hand for a surgeon or dentist, or outstanding brushwork skills for a portrait painter, are examples. Then there are the more cerebral skills, such as use of language, problem solving and mathematical ability, all vital to so many jobs, and together making up, in large part, the more traditional ability known as intelligence, and measured as intelligence quotient (IQ). But there is yet another set of personal characteristics that are not actually essential if we have to design a bridge, or complete a project on time and on budget. But they do make it considerably easier to do any job, and get on with people at work in the process; and, in so doing, this inevitably will have a positive effect on productivity and on the quality of your experience and achievements in the workplace.

These kinds of skills and characteristics are those that help us to succeed in life and get on with other people, especially at work. They include being easy to get on with, being able to read people well, and being generally 'emotionally aware', both for yourself and others. Collectively, these and other similar characteristics have become known as 'emotional intelligence', to equate their importance with, but distinguish them from, the more cerebral IQ. So, your emotional intelligence quotient, or emotional IQ, is definitely a relevant concept for this book.

Emotional IQ isn't just about 'being in touch with your feelings' or being able to 'talk about your feelings' (not that there is anything wrong with that), but these phrases have often been used in a pejorative sense, when discussing what are sometimes called the 'softer skills'. What emotional IQ does is value aspects of our behaviour other than those traditionally associated with intelligence (and measured mainly by language and mathematical skills), because there is so much more than IQ playing a part in defining how well we perform on workplace tasks.

What is important here, though, in terms of building self-confidence, is that, whereas our abilities in the traditional IQ are, to a large extent, innate, the abilities that make up emotional IQ can be learned and practised, and so improved. And the good news is that, much of what we've already covered in earlier chapters, and will be covering in Chapters 7 and 8, will give you direct guidance on how to improve those skills that contribute to Emotional IQ.

Measure your emotional intelligence quotient

So, let's discover how emotionally intelligent you are. I've arranged the scoring on this activity to produce a figure that can be roughly compared with IQ, that has an average figure of 100, and the very highest scores of around 140.

For each of these characteristics, rate yourself on the scale below, and write down your scores in your personal journal:

Poor	09
Average	10
Fairly good	11
Good	12
Very good	13
Excellent	14

Characteristic	Description
1. Emotional awareness	Being aware of your own and others' feelings, and being able to read these and have an idea of what has brought these about.
2. Problem solving	Seeing problems and coming up with possible solutions.
3. Independence	Managing most things without outside support or help, but knowing when to ask for help.
4. Emotional self-expression	The ability to show appropriate emotions at the right time.
5. Self-actualisation	The ability to have meaningful goals for yourself and set about achieving them.
6. Flexibility	Being aware that change can happen and being ready to adapt to this; the ability to try new things.
7. Social responsibility	Cooperating with others and making a contribution of your time or skills for the greater good.
8. Impulse control	Being patient when it's needed, resisting temptation and not acting on impulse.
9. Decision making	Considering options, weighing these up and reaching a decision.
10. Interpersonal relationships	Having a positive attitude and developing strong relationships involving trust and mutual benefit.

When you've finished, add up your score to give you your emotional IQ. As with IQ, an average score on this scale would be 100.

Here is a guide to what your emotional IQ score means:

90–95	poor
96–105	average
106–115	quite good
116–125	good
126–135	very good
136–140	excellent

Now look over your lowest scoring items and check out the parts of the book that refer to this, so that you can work on improving these – use the contents list or the index as a guide.

Chill time

Your special relaxed place

Think of a place where you always feel relaxed and at ease. Maybe on holiday, at home, wherever. Now close your eyes, and imagine yourself in that place in as much detail and as vividly as you can. Use all your senses to make the image stronger. Spend a few seconds or a few minutes in your special relaxed place whenever you need to relax mind and body.

Managing and being managed

Much of the preparatory work we do in order to get the job we want, is concerned with acquiring the necessary skills for the day-to-day work we will be doing, from selling to teaching to diagnosing patients, to administration, analysing data, developing software, and everything in between. But, what many of us have not yet learned on our first day at work, is how to manage and how to be managed. And yet, this is an intrinsic part of our working life. First being managed, and then possibly moving on to managing others, too.

Wherever you are in the workplace hierarchy, all that's gone before in this and earlier chapters will have much that can help you to feel more confident, whether managing or being managed. Chapters 7 and 8 will also include relevant material.

Career progression in most workplaces involves taking on a management role. But, although being a manager can seem daunting, there is much you can do to broaden your skill base while you are waiting to finally achieve that promotion. Despite what you may believe, being a good manager is something that rarely comes naturally.

Though there is tremendous variation, most management that works well is a blend of the 'softer' emotionally intelligent skills, such as supportive exchange, empathy, being able to motivate, and so on (which I'll explain further just shortly), with the 'harder' skills of making sure a job gets done well and on time, and supervising and organising a team of people.

Understanding management brings confidence

No matter what your working role, understanding the role of the manager will give you a better foundation for being more self-confident. Managing others, or being managed, is a hotbed of possibilities for making people lose confidence in themselves. Many of the clients I coach are struggling with confidence issues because they can't understand their manager's attitude and have blamed themselves for having shortcomings, when really the problem was with their manager, whose management skills were poor. Likewise, I've coached managers who were just handed the job with no training and no real understanding of how to manage, and were just stumbling along doing what they thought was best.

Whether manager or managed (or both), the best way to improve your confidence is to get to know the source of the problem better. Knowledge is power, and so is understanding. So, learn more about being a manager. Find out where your manager is coming from. This usually explains a lot. As Sun Tzu, the Chinese philosopher, said thousands of years ago, 'Know thy self, know thy enemy'.

You can do this by:

1. **Observing or finding out what the accepted management style is in your workplace**. Then check out the jargon that's being used, and read up on it. Management today is usually (but not always) more about consultation and collaboration, flexibility and cooperation, and not at all about 'Do this, and do that, because I said so'.

2. **Reading up on alternative management styles**, especially if there is no accepted style in your workplace. This aids your overall understanding, but also allows you to choose which you would prefer to use, if it's up to you.

3. **Checking out the company website**, or any other public documents, to learn about its main aims and objectives, and current priorities. This will tell you a lot about the pressure from above acting on company managers and decision makers all the way up to the Board room.

4. **Continuing to develop your skills** and maintaining your knowledge and understanding of the company management structure.

Your own management style will depend on many factors, including the ethos and practices in your workplace, the training you've had, your personality, managers you've seen in action (one way or another) and the background skills and experience you bring to the table. Management style is a fluid and changing concept in practice, and it makes sense to keep up to speed and be one step ahead of the game.

DON'T FORGET

The good stress myth

Let me lay to rest an unfortunate misunderstanding, which most people have heard, that there is 'good stress and bad stress'. You might as well say there are good colds and bad colds, or a good broken leg and a bad broken leg. This idea makes no sense, but has been accepted and expounded for over 50 years now. It has also led to many managers feeling that it's OK to pile on demands and stress on their workforce, in the mistaken belief that this is good for them, and that productivity and efficiency will improve. Wrong, wrong, wrong.

(More on this, and on stress in Chapter 7.)

Preparing to become a manager with confidence

By failing to prepare, you are preparing to fail.

Benjamin Franklin, founding father of the United States, 1706–90

These famous words are often quoted, and they hit the nail right on the head here. You wouldn't aim to be a lawyer, an architect or a doctor without taking the necessary training, and gaining relevant experience. And yet, people walk straight into management roles every day without any kind of preparation at all. This isn't because they are hasty and unwise. It's just because it's what most people do. Being able to manage others tends to be seen as a basic skill, or even as part of your personality, and not something you should train and prepare for. And yet this is such an important and pivotal role in any workplace, affecting both the manager and the managed deeply, and with huge implications for the success of the business.

So, to succeed in management, even if you feel it may not be for you, here's what you can be doing to prepare:

➡ Follow the same suggestions given in the previous section.

➡ Then, choose the style to go for, and be confident enough in yourself to ask if there is a *course* you could take on this, or if you could link up with a *mentor* to show you the ropes – this also shows you're keen and will be a plus when it comes to selecting candidates for career progression.

➡ Well ahead, build and *keep a good rapport with your own line manager*, others in management and other team leaders, as they will be good sources of information and support while you are preparing, and when you eventually move up to lead your own team.

Most common complaints about managers

Whether manager or managed, bear in mind these recent findings about staff reports on the key drawbacks in their managers:

➡ Poor communication skills.

➡ Making staff feel threatened rather than rewarded.

➡ Being over-stressed.

➡ Disorganised or forgetful.

➡ Micromanagement.

➡ Not recognising effort and contribution, but quick to criticise.

→ Not explaining the benefits of, or reasons for, changes or restructuring.

→ Caring more about what employees did, than how they were feeling.

→ Lack of empathy.

DON'T FORGET

Stay true to yourself

Keep a tight hold on your self-image and sense of identity. It's easy to lose sense of who you are, and those traits and qualities that make you who you are when you begin to use new techniques to improve your communication with other people. Remember that staying true to yourself is just as important, and being genuine matters. It's particularly relevant here, as it is so important that you continue to be yourself, and that you are exactly what you appear to be.

Genuineness is a kind of 'what you see is what you get' characteristic. And, how you stay true to yourself and remain a genuine person, is by taking all you're learning in this book on board, slowly and carefully. Practise and try out your new skills, just as you would with anything else you were learning, before using them for real. Build them piece by piece into your own way of being, so that they strengthen your identity and confidence.

Opportunities multiply, as they are seized.

Sun Tzu, ancient Chinese philosopher, 544–496 BCE

➡ Different situations are suited to different communication styles, such as small talk, social conversation and supportive exchange.

➡ Active listening is a key skill in supportive exchanges.

➡ Getting on with people is easier if you use open, rather than closed, questions and statements.

➡ Empathy is the ability to understand what it feels like in another person's position.

➡ Empathy is a key part of active listening, supportive exchanges and building rapport.

➡ A warm tone of voice, open posture and good eye contact make for good communication, whatever the situation.

➡ Establishing a rapport with colleagues at whatever level makes for a better working environment and also provides the potential for mentoring and networking opportunities.

➡ Skills, such as empathy, emotional awareness, motivating others, impulse control and independence, make up emotional intelligence, which can improve performance at work, can all be learned and practised.

➡ Being able to manage others can also be learned and prepared for. It is a blend of the 'softer' skills of emotional intelligence with the more practical and cerebral skills of planning, problem solving, decision making, overseeing others and getting things done.

Chapter seven

How to be more resilient

What you'll learn in this chapter:	This will help you to be more confident in any work situation, especially:
1. How to become more resilient to stress.	1. Team meetings/'morning huddle'.
2. How to relax mind and body and give/receive a relaxing shoulder massage.	2. Giving a talk or presentation, making a report or running a training session at any level.
3. How to cope better with your own feelings, such as anger, panic or taking things personally or too seriously.	3. Communication at all levels (including letter, e-mail and phone) up to Board level.
4. How to get back into the swing of it after a break.	4. Work-related social or team building events.
5. How to improve your general well-being.	5. Changing demands and stressors.

This chapter will provide you with powerful skills and techniques that will build your resilience for situations at work that might shake your confidence. In other words, this chapter will explore ways to cushion yourself so that you are affected less, rather like an air bag in a car, or knee and elbow pads for skateboarding. First, one of the most common confidence shakers – stress.

What is stress anyway?

We all know what stress is, but try explaining it in a few sentences ... it's really difficult. It's not that it's particularly complicated, it's more that it's hard to put it into words, especially without experiencing it first hand, as I certainly have. It's a bit like love or pain – you'll know it when you feel it, but it's hard to describe exactly what it is. The reason for that is probably the same – that stress is a combination of emotional and physical sensations. Anyway, here is what I find the best way to explain stress. I sidestep what it is for now, and describe when we're likely to feel it.

At its simplest, you feel stressed when there is a feeling of unpleasant and unwanted pressure because of circumstances that make you feel one or more of these:

➡ threatened;

➡ unsure or unfamiliar;

➡ overwhelmed;

➡ trapped;

➡ dissatisfied or unhappy;

➡ that you can't cope as well as you want to;

➡ that you can't cope at all.

Though this is a definition of stress, it reads just like a description of what it feels like to lack confidence. So, it's not surprising that low confidence goes hand in hand with stress. The thing is, stress doesn't come with a label, so often we'll label it in some other way, depending on how exactly we experience it – anything from tension, to fear, anxiety, panic, stress, nervousness, no confidence, scared, and so on.

As stress is a key feature in this chapter, there will be some extra 'Chill times' for you to try – beginning with this one.

Give or receive a relaxing scalp or neck and shoulders massage

If you have a willing friend or partner, massaging either the scalp or the shoulders and neck can help relax your entire body. You can give or receive this, and both participants should find it relaxing. Start with gentle, short, broad strokes, with flattened fingers, to warm up the whole area to be massaged. Then, still with flat fingers, use slower, longer and more gliding strokes, and light to medium pressure to release tension. If the pressure used could just crush a ripe grape under your fingers, you've got it just about right.

Taking the sting out of stress

Almost everyone knows what it feels like to be stressed, even if it's for the few hours before an exam, a driving test, during a job interview or an appraisal. Maybe you have been lucky and have never felt stressed, so you might be tempted to skip this section. Don't! Most of the ideas and thoughts about stress given here will also be helpful in increasing your confidence. That's because stress and low self-confidence are either end of a two-way street. Feeling stressed makes your confidence level fall. And lacking confidence produces stress. And, anyway, sometimes you're the last to know that you're stressed – so keep reading!

STRESS ⇄ LACK OF CONFIDENCE

Stress is notoriously badly explained, because it is quite easy to misunderstand many aspects of stress and then pass this misunderstanding on to others. Also the internet has allowed many misunderstandings to go viral and be repeated over and over. This applies to every subject, not just stress. So, you may have heard some myths about stress that just aren't true. Just because it's in an article or book about stress, in a website or online discussion, doesn't make it true. I'll be busting those myths in this chapter. Sadly, the legislation that makes sure that advertising doesn't mislead us does not extend to articles, websites, information leaflets and downloads, books and documentaries, or even the news! Whatever topic you're looking for on the internet, or you hear about on a news broadcast, and especially if the subject is stress, pay attention to the following:

➡ Always check who is saying what you're reading or hearing, and what their background is. Are they independent? Was the study or evidence collection valid, robust and reliable?

➡ The news and current affairs media will often report what has been said by an organisation or individual, sometimes on flimsy evidence or from a particular standpoint, and that's perfectly legitimate, but if you haven't caught the short introductory phrase, 'According to …' you could absorb the report as confirmed fact.

➡ Look at the original source or evidence for yourself – many misinterpretations and plain incorrect data and information is repeated again and again, through the power of cut and paste, with no one ever checking out the original source.

➡ Wikipedia is a wonderful source of information, but bear in mind it has not been independently verified, and anyone can add material to it.

Obstacles are those frightful things you see when you take your eyes off your goal.

Henry Ford, founder of the Ford Motor Company, 1863–1947

Why stress makes you feel bad

When your brain registers that you are experiencing stress, whether minor or major, the stress hormones, adrenalin and cortisol are automatically released to help you to cope with whatever is stressing you. This changes your body's normal finely tuned chemical balance, which is usually working in the background on its default everyday setting without you having to raise a finger. You don't have to tell your heart to beat, your lungs to breathe, or your bladder to produce urine, and so on. It all just happens.

But when your brain has registered that you are feeling unable to cope with a stressor, it turns the dial up to 'under attack', and alters all your default settings according to the level of threat. This would be fine if you were in physical danger, which this reflex action was designed for, in stone age times. You would be beautifully prepared to run away really fast, lift heavy objects, if one had fallen on you or a loved one, or to fight with a predator or hostile tribe. But here's the rub. Though this reflex action is still a lifesaver in cases of accidents or other physical threats and dangers, stress at work is usually of a psychosocial nature. In other words, it's when you feel a threat to you as a person. Your brain can't tell the difference and presses the 'red alert' button, whether you've just stepped into the path of a car, or you've just realised you're not going to make that vital deadline.

Here are just some of the other reasons for stress at work:

long hours	juggling family and job
being overloaded	incompetence in others
tight deadlines	working conditions
difficult people	isolation
job insecurity	conflict with others

role uncertainty	always on duty
being a workaholic	the responsibility
business problems	moving home a lot
bullying	poor communication
constant change	being away from home a lot
low pay	unlikely promotion
shift work	lack of confidence
travel to work	lack of control
demands on home life	noise/heat/cold

So, your body has prepared you for intense physical action, but there you are sitting in a meeting, at a desk, on the way home in the car or on a train. So, as you would expect, your body is in turmoil, all geared up to run for your life, but with nowhere to go. And this produces many physical symptoms, as well as changes in your usual behaviour and thinking processes, which you experience as the symptoms of stress – raised heart rate, increased breathing rate, changes to your thinking processes, anger, panic, and all the rest. And this can be very scary, if you are carrying out your everyday work tasks. So, your brain reacts by producing yet more stress reaction, more symptoms, you feel even more scared, and so on into a vicious circle, which can feel very, very unpleasant indeed. The end result can be a 'panic attack', which I'll explain shortly.

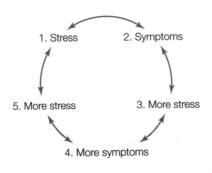

How stressed are you?

Here are just some of the ways stress can make you feel. You are unlikely to experience them all but, on the other hand, just one may suggest stress.

Physical	Emotional	Behaviour
Dry mouth	Panicky	Lack of concentration
Churning stomach	Irritable	Restless
Tiredness	Forgetful	Unable to sleep or very sleepy
Unwanted muscle tension	'Unreal'	Eating too much or too little
Trembling	Anxious	Making mistakes
Diarrhoea	Worried	Change in usual behaviour
Sweating	Depressed	Indecisive
Heart racing	Negative	Forgetful
	Sad	

What to do

1. Use your personal journal to record which of these you have experienced/felt *more often than not in the past seven days*.

2. Now give a score to each item recorded, from 1 to 5, to express how severely you feel that symptom, 1 being slightly, 5 being as bad as it can possibly get.

3. Add up your score.

0	no stress
1–9	probably overtired
10–19	overtired or slightly stressed
20–39	slightly stressed
40–69	moderately stressed
70–99	very stressed
100–125	highly stressed

Myth 1: Some stress is good for you

Saying that 'a little stress is good for you' is like saying breaking a toe is good for you, but breaking a leg is bad. This idea makes no sense, and yet it has been accepted by many major organisations for decades. A serious outcome of this myth has been that many employers have felt justified in placing their workforce under stress, believing this is good for them, and that productivity and efficiency will improve. This has contributed in no small way to the huge increases in stress over those same decades.

This myth of there being 'good' stress, or 'eustress', came about because we all perform better at work when we are absorbed and enthused by it. Unfortunately, some decades ago, largely because of the misinterpretation of some early research, this positive idea became confused with the negative one of 'stress' and the concept of 'good stress and bad stress' was born, along with the pernicious idea that we all need a bit of stress to perform well.

DON'T FORGET

Organisations such as the Health and Safety Executive (HSE) have recently recognised this mix-up and are taking the revised stance that all stress is unpleasant and 'bad', and that people feel better and work better when they have the optimum level of positive challenge, stimulation, enthusiasm, motivation and interest in their work, but are not 'stressed'. If what you are feeling is positive and motivating, it isn't stress.

Stress is the adverse reaction people have to excessive pressures or other types of demand placed on them at work.

HSE's formal definition of work related stress, 2013

How you can develop your resilience to stress

As I said earlier, there is so much misinformation and ideas straight off the top of someone's head for you to find on the internet, from friends, magazines, and so-called 'experts'. But there are also solid, reliable and fully researched findings on how best to cope with stress, and here they are – I'll explain these in more detail next.

➡ Can you do anything about the cause of your stress?

➡ Slow down and make time for quick and easy relaxation techniques.

➡ Use quick and easy breathing techniques.

➡ Take breaks – daily, weekly and yearly.

➡ Use time in a way that meets your needs well.

➡ Live a lifestyle that promotes health and well-being and builds resilience.

➡ Recognise and deal with panic attacks.

➡ Think yourself calm.

➡ Be as active as you can.

Can you do anything about the cause of your stress?

This is the first question to ask yourself when you feel stressed. Because the most obvious, but often forgotten, way to cope better with stress is to remove the cause of it altogether. The reason this is often missed is that most stress-ors are beyond your power to change them. But sometimes you may be able to at least reduce the extent of the problem. So, your first step will always be to decide whether you can actually reduce or remove the reason for the stress.

1. **If you think you can**. Go for it. You can also find someone with the expertise to advise you about it, if that would help. This would apply to bullying and harassment, and discrimination of any kind, or difficulties with a colleague. Use the channels provided and seek out whatever support is available to you to do this, whether in the workplace or outside of it. All these are common difficulties, it's not just you, so no one will be surprised or shocked. But, also, do all you can to cushion yourself from its effects, and build your resilience too, as explained in this chapter.

2. **If you're not sure**. Find expert advice and support to help clarify the situation – a chat with an objective and supportive expert third party can help you see what the main issues really are and what, if anything, you can do to improve the situation.

3. **If you are still unsure** why you feel stressed, it is probably because of your general approach to life or business, and this whole chapter, and the entire book, should help you explore this and find ways forward.

Slow down and make time for relaxation

The pace of life is extremely fast, and most people constantly juggle numerous bits of information in their heads. Your body and mind need a break from this, in order to function at their best. How you choose to relax is very much down to your preferences. But allowing your body to completely chill out at least once every day soothes your nervous system and builds resilience. A quiet walk, relaxing music, a lazy bath, gardening or a run are just a few ways you can do this. Special relaxation techniques are also really useful because they can be done more quickly than most of these, and you can usually fit them into your day anywhere, and in any situation. You'll find these in the 'Chill time' boxes in every chapter to try out and use.

Chill time

Web and tech

In addition to the quick and easy relaxation techniques throughout this book, there is a huge choice of ways of relaxing and keeping tabs on your stress available on the internet, via software or an app. There's everything from the humble Biodot and screensaver, to massage chairs, sophisticated monitors and software packages. New resources come online every day. Some are free and some have a cost, from a few pounds to several hundred.

Take your breath away

As discussed before, stress shows in your breathing. The change may be slight and unnoticeable to you, but stress speeds up your breathing rate, even just by a few extra breaths a minute. You'll also find yourself breathing less deeply and with the top part of your chest, compared to the more usual and more relaxed abdominal breathing. Even small changes to breathing alters body chemistry and how you feel, and this happens within minutes, if not seconds. Feeling faint, tingling in your fingers, poor concentration, indecision and your mind going blank can all be signs of breathing a little faster or 'overbreathing'. So breathing normally can help to relieve many of the symptoms of stress and will also help reduce tension and anxiety, and just make you feel more content.

Myth 2: Take deep breaths, it will calm you down

How often do you hear someone being told to take deep breaths when they are uptight? Most people, when asked, would probably agree that taking deep breaths is good for you. But no, it's natural, normal breathing that's good for you. Taking lots of deep abdominal breaths can cause panic attacks, angina pain, back pain and other problems. Breathing that is concentrated in the upper chest and/or is too fast, even by a few breaths per second, upsets the body chemistry's delicate balance. So, normal automatic breathing is best, and practise the breathing techniques that you'll find in the 'Chill time' boxes throughout the book, using these if you are feeling stressed.

Don't let time push you around

The stress messengers in our blood make us rush everything. We talk quickly, eat quickly, work for too long and 'fire fight' or crisis manage much of the time, instead of planning ahead and thinking things out properly. With home commitments on top, clock watching becomes a way of life, and this is exacerbated by 24/7 contact from everyone. You can begin to feel that the clock is controlling your life. Much of this we do without thinking because our body is already stressed and is pushing us in all the wrong directions. However, the upshot usually is that mistakes are made, work can need redoing, decisions made can be poor, and quality suffers, all of which means that more time is needed to complete work to the required standard, making all the rushing truly counterproductive.

These are some of the ways you can take back control of the clock:

- ➡ Be organised and know where everything is.

- ➡ Don't set unreasonably tight deadlines for yourself – you are often the one who does this to yourself (I know I do) – so cut yourself some slack.

- ➡ Do one job at a time whenever possible.

- ➡ Keep lists of jobs to be done, separating urgent and non-urgent.

- ➡ Select and prioritise what you do – you can't do it all – delegate whenever possible.

- ➡ Say 'no' when you should (how to do this is in Chapter 3).

- ➡ Plan your days and weeks in advance and keep a diary.

DON'T FORGET

Whatever the problem at work – remember, you can take control, and you can do something about it.

Myth 3: If I skip lunch, I'll get more done

A common automatic reaction to time pressure is to miss out on your breaks. We've all done it. Coffee and a doughnut from the machine or coffee shop while you work. Eat lunch at your desk, while you're shopping, driving or walking to your next important place to be. It makes some kind of sense, as you can get more done and meet that deadline, or get to that appointment on time. OK so far. If it's just for today. But, if this style of working slips into happening on more days than not or, worse, every day, then your system won't be able to take it in its stride and your body and mind will begin to suffer for it.

Skipping breaks is one of those counter-intuitive choices. No, you don't get more done if you skip lunch and your afternoon tea break, even if you drink lots of coffee or high-energy drinks to keep you going, or grab a sandwich on the go. Not if it isn't the exception, but the rule. Apart from the health issues related to irregular eating, and too much caffeine, your body will be working well below par for most of the day due to tiredness and, if you haven't eaten for hours, or you fill up on high-sugar foods, your blood sugar levels will be well below the optimum for any kind of task, or varying wildly, and your concentration, memory and problem-solving abilities will drop more and more as each hour goes by.

But, if you take regular breaks and eat properly, over the average day, you'll get more done and it will be done better. And think how much better you'll feel, too. You know it makes sense. Even a five-minute complete break in a stressful morning can work wonders. I can certainly vouch for that, and the research bears this out, too.

DON'T FORGET

Stress is not always connected to bad things. Even 'happy' events, such as a hard-won new job, a new baby or buying a new house, can be very stressful. This is because even good things usually involve change, and lots to be done, both of which are stressful. And, on top of that, there are always anxieties and concerns that everything will turn out well.

Life is for living to the full

You don't have to be a punch bag and just take the stresses and strains of life. You can prepare yourself for them. You can create cushioning or a shield by building your resilience. Many simple adjustments to the way we live our lives can make stress easier to cope with. Here are some of these. Note in your journal any you think might work for you, and try them when you feel the time is right:

➡ Eat regularly. Don't skip meals, especially breakfast and lunch.

➡ Avoid too much food or drink containing caffeine, e.g. energy drinks, some flu or headache remedies, cola, coffee, chocolate (sorry!).

➡ Eat a healthy and well-balanced diet.

➡ Do things you enjoy regularly – 'me-time' is a must. It's not selfish, everyone around you will benefit from a happier, more relaxed you. So make time for enjoyable hobbies, interests and leisure pursuits, or just for doing nothing.

➡ Don't rely on alcohol or other substances to help you sleep or relax.

➡ Plenty of restful sleep works wonders – relaxation and breathing techniques help if you can't get off to sleep, or you wake up during the night.

➡ If you have a late night, allow time to catch up on missed sleep.

➡ Regular physical activity that fits in with your commitments and is something you enjoy, will produce calmness and a sense of well-being. Even if you are initially really unenthusiastic, the feel-good factor cuts in very quickly, after only 5 or 10 minutes of activity.

It's not difficult to build activity into your life without going to a gym, or signing up for a course. Here are some easy ways to make your days more active, while you're at work:

➡ Offer to help with jobs that involve activity.

➡ Walk up the stairs rather than taking the lift whenever you can.

➡ Try walking over to see a colleague at the other end of the building, rather than sending them an e-mail or phoning.

➡ Have a 'walking meeting', instead of a seated one.

➡ When out in the car, park a bit further away than you need to, and walk the extra distance.

➡ On the bus, get off a stop early.

Chill time

Relaxing by numbers

Slowly and silently count down the numbers from 10 to 0 and, with each downward count, imagine yourself unwinding, releasing tension, letting go and relaxing your entire body a little bit more. Repeat once or twice as necessary.

Panic attacks can be handled

Stress can bring on sudden attacks of particularly acute anxiety or panic. Seeming to appear from nowhere, they then decline and disappear again, lasting anything from several minutes, to half an hour at most. The first thing you feel is your stomach turning over or churning, or your heart racing. You might feel hot and sweaty, light-headed and very fearful, with an urgent need to escape. Others find themselves rooted to the spot, simply unable to move, no matter how much they try. Panic attacks are the body's full-blown emergency 'fight, flight or freeze' reaction, which happens completely automatically when we are in extreme physical danger to give us the energy and muscle strength to help us either to run away from or fight whatever is threatening us. Just as some animals will freeze to prevent attack, this can happen to some people, too. These attacks lasts a maximum of 20 minutes because your body can't sustain the reaction for any longer. 'Fight, flight or freeze' is a very ancient, primitive, but life-saving part of us. If you had to take the time to work out what to do if a pedestrian steps out in front of your car, it could already be too late. The 'fight or flight' reaction does it for you before you even have time to blink.

If you have experienced a panic attack, or a generally panicky feeling, you've probably found that just telling yourself to pull yourself together and not panic doesn't work very well. I mentioned earlier that the panic response is set off automatically, like breathing or your heart beating. You can't tell your heart to stop beating, either. However, physical techniques like the 'PAUSE Technique' can reach and turn off this automatic response.

The PAUSE Technique for panic attacks

When you're gripped by panic, it's really hard to think straight. That's what the 'PAUSE Technique' is all about. It's specially designed to make it easy to remember just what to do, in the midst of panic.

So, the letters P A U S E spell out what to do, and remembering the word PAUSE gets you started. Using this very straightforward technique will stop the panic attack going any further, and makes it less likely to happen again. For many people, it works the first time. But, for others, it can take a bit of practice. However, with a bit of determination, it can work for you. It gives you back control over something that seemed uncontrollable.

If you have a panic attack, or begin to feel panicky, the trick is to catch this early, and stop it there. Here is what to do. When you notice your first signs of an imminent panic attack:

Pause ... and make yourself comfortable

Absorb ... detail of what's going on around you ▶

Use … any method of relaxing quickly that works well for you, *then*

Slowly … when you feel better,

Ease … yourself back into what you were doing.

Calm and relaxed thinking

Sometimes it's your mind that just won't relax. Even with a relaxed body, it is possible for the mind to be stressing away on its own, worrying about this, fretting about that, and thinking 'what if …' almost anything. This can be the most annoying and wearing experience. Being able to relax physically goes some way to relaxing your mind. But sometimes a bit more is needed to do the trick.

Simply telling yourself not to think about something, or to take your mind off your worries, will achieve little. It's a bit like telling the automatic pilot on a flight to slow down. It just won't hear you. No, the key tip here is that the way to get your mind off your worries is to give your mind something else to think about. And the way to make it relax is to give it something relaxing to think about. Chapters 5–8 include Chill times' specially designed to help you to relax your mind. And here are some others to try, so that you can find one that works for you.

Chill time for the mind

Mental pictures

To relax your mind, first relax your body as much as possible (use any of the book's relaxation techniques). Then try these procedures to find which works best for you. Spend from one to three minutes on any one method.

Focal point 1

Focus your mind absolutely on one of these:

➡ A calming poem or prayer.

➡ A well-loved face or picture.

Focal point 2

Repeat silently (or quietly) and very slowly a word or phrase such as:

➡ Relax.

➡ My mind is quiet and peaceful.

➡ I'm letting go and relaxing.

Mind's eye pictures

Imagine yourself in one of the following settings in as much detail and as clearly and vividly as you can:

➡ By the ocean as the waves roll in and out, in and out, feel the spray, hear the sounds, smell the salt in the air.

➡ Relaxing on a fluffy cloud, drifting along in a blue sky, and warmed from above by a shining sun.

Choose your words carefully

The words used when you think, and your attitudes and basic beliefs, can also contribute much to how stressed you feel. In Chapter 2, we explored many examples of this, such as using words like 'should' or 'must', tending to blame yourself when things go wrong, or taking a negative perspective on life. The focus was on the kind of 'inner dialogue' people have with themselves every day, and how that might affect levels of stress and tension. We all have a kind of 'running commentary' going on in our heads, and it can often be negative and discouraging. But, once you're aware this is going on, and the consequences, it becomes possible to change it.

As a reminder, here are some of the key areas covered in Chapter 2, as all of these can help you to build your resilience to stress:

➡ Some common thoughts, assumptions and beliefs (TABs) can be unhelpful in that they limit your achievement and lower your self-confidence.

➡ Becoming aware of these TABs and challenging them can remove or reduce this effect.

➡ Replacing these TABs with positive versions can improve self-confidence and achievement.

➡ Being mindful for at least five minutes a day can boost self-confidence. You can be mindful if you bring your thoughts into the here and now, slow down and quietly use your senses to take everything in around you, feeling and experiencing the moment fully.

➡ Visualising yourself dealing calmly and confidently with a situation several times before it happens can really improve your performance.

Be active!

Choose activities or exercise you really enjoy. Exercise doesn't have to be boring to do you good! And, if it fits in easily with your lifestyle, so much the better. So choose activities that make you feel good, don't rush into anything you're not ready for, and you'll find that all these benefits of regular exercise are very real. Exercise:

- → takes your mind off any anxieties;
- → releases 'endorphins' in the brain, which have the effect of enhancing your sense of well-being;
- → sends a refreshing and energising blood flow around the whole body;
- → helps you to sleep better;
- → eases unwanted muscle tension;
- → gives you more energy;
- → improves overall health, well-being and general resilience.

DON'T FORGET

Check with your doctor if you're not sure of your fitness before beginning any exercise or activity. If you're new to exercise, or it's been a while, it's best to sign up for a course or join a club so that there's someone there to guide you.

My 20 best strategies for building resilience to stress

1. Scan your body for stress and tension regularly each day.
2. Share your troubles with a good, trusted support network.
3. Relax mind and body some time every day, for at least five minutes. Do this several times a day during a stressful period.
4. Aim for a lifestyle that includes regular enjoyable exercise, leisure time, and 'me-time'.
5. Eat healthily, avoid too much caffeine and don't skip meals.
6. Know that you are not a victim and that you can take control and make changes to improve things.
7. Take regular breaks and get a good night's sleep.
8. Avoid hurry and rushing. Live your life at a liveable speed.

9. Don't use alcohol or non-prescription drugs to combat stress or disappointment.

10. Don't give up easily. Know that sometimes all that's needed is a bit of effort.

11. Approach life with a positive attitude.

12. Recognise that you have inner strength and varied skills, talents and abilities.

13. Know that you can think through and find solutions to problems.

14. Respect your own needs and those of others, know how to compromise and say no when you want to.

15. Know that everyone can make mistakes and know how to learn from them.

16. Have friends who are positive and supportive.

17. Accept offers of help and ask for help when needed. There is no need to make life hard for yourself. And people love to help.

18. Work out your priorities and be organised – know where you are, where you want to go and how you plan to get there.

19. Have a sense of humour and be able to laugh at yourself sometimes.

20. Have a sense of purpose – know what it is and how to follow it.

Too sensitive for your own good? How not to take things personally

You may be surprised to hear this, but it's OK to be sensitive. You may well think that there can't be a positive side to being sensitive. Here's an activity that might help you to start to change your mind.

In action

How sensitive are you?

1. First, find a new page in your journal and write your name at the top left-hand-side.

2. Now, on a scale of 0 (having no sensitivity at all) to 100 (being as sensitive as possible), give yourself a rating for, say, the past month, and write this beside your name.

3. Next, think about colleagues (past or present) you admire most or really like. Still on the same side of your sheet of paper, write down their names underneath your own (perhaps use initials if others may read your journal). Four or five should be enough, but the more the better. Now give them a score on the same sensitivity scale. Take your time and really think about it. Be honest!

4. How does your score compare with the others? Higher? Lower? About the same?

The chances are that the people you have chosen, like you, are scoring fairly high on sensitivity. Most of the people we like and admire in this world rate quite highly on the sensitivity meter. Now, why should that be? I shall explain. Here are two typical sensitive people and some of their experiences.

Sharon

Sometimes Sharon finds life lets her down. She can't seem to get through a week without feeling a little hurt by something said or done by one of her colleagues. This is really getting to her. But Sharon always has an open door for any of her team, who find her an effective and reliable team leader. She's a great listener, intuitive yet analytical, and could quickly pinpoint where a problem lay, and then discuss ways forward.

The practice manager is always complaining to Phil, an experienced GP, about running late with his appointments. This really bothers Phil. But what is he to do? As for all GPs, many of his patients are stressed or feeling down, and he can't just ignore that, can he? This takes longer than tonsillitis or a rash to deal with properly. And, if he rushes things, they'll just be back the next week, feeling worse. In his practice, most patients see Phil as a really good doctor, who helps you feel much better. There is often a bit of a wait to see him, but most patients feel it's worth it.

Sharon and Phil's experiences show us just some of the ways that being sensitive can and does work for you. Because with being sensitive comes a whole other package of characteristics that you may have and be happy to have.

You may not have been aware of it, but you probably have some or all of the following list of positive characteristics. Don't be modest, really think about each of these. Which would you say apply to you? Be honest with yourself:

Caring	Committed
Intuitive	Analytical
Perceptive	Deep thinker
Likeable	Very good at seeing other people's
Alert	point of view
Empathic	Aware of subtleties
Good listener	Can visualise different scenarios
Reliable	Aware of consequences

You may have been aware of this positive side of sensitivity, but have discounted its importance because you tend to focus on what you see as the more negative, sensitive side. You may feel that being sensitive is what defines you. But is that logical?

➡ Do you throw out all of the fruit in a bowl if one apple is mouldy?

➡ Would you scrap a car with a flat tyre?

➡ Do you judge a garden by one weed in a corner?

➡ Does your impression of a whole room depend on one picture on one wall?

I cannot give you the formula for success, but I can give you the formula for failure – which is: try to please everybody.

Herbert Swope, American newspaper editor, 1882–1958

So what can you do about the negative side of being sensitive?

➡ Take on board all aspects of being sensitive, not just bits of it. Being sensitive is pretty much a prerequisite for being a caring and intuitive person and many of the other characteristics listed above. These characteristics may be a source of inspiration and admiration to other people. They may be the aspects of you that you like, too!

➡ Use every other chapter in this book (and especially Chapters 2 and 3) to help you not to feel hurt by the comments or actions of others.

➡ Focus less on the negative side of being sensitive and make sure to harness and really use the much more substantial positive side.

➡ Another way to look at this is to think of people you know who aren't sensitive. Think of people who have very little or no sensitivity at all. They are likely to be more self-centred than you, and likely to make more tactless comments than you, with or without realising it. They may well be the very people you feel hurt by.

➡ You really can't please all the people all the time, so don't give yourself such a hard time for being just like everyone else.

➡ We all have days when we're more or less sensitive than others, due to variations in mood, hormones, how tired we are, what happened the day before, and so on.

Returning to work after a break

Coming back from a long time sick, a period of unemployment, or from maternity leave can be a real confidence drainer. Everything seems to have changed, nothing seems familiar, there will be new faces, and everyone expects you just to slot right back in, even though you feel like you're starting all over again. And, as if that wasn't enough, you've lost the work routine, as you may have spent long hours alone, or coping with small children, and feel your brain needs time to click into place and change gear. You may even worry if it ever will again.

Yes, it may take a few weeks to reacquaint yourself with your workplace and the changes that have taken place – but there's no need to apologise for that. Everyone goes through this at some time, and most will fully understand your position. So, just ask someone if you need to know something, and you'll quickly be back up to speed. Or try dropping in for a few visits in the weeks before you return to update yourself, or perhaps fire off some e-mails to colleagues to get a feel for goings-on and get back in the loop. It makes sense and shows enthusiasm, energy and forward thinking, all good skills to show off to your line manager and colleagues.

Returning after sick leave

If you're returning after weeks or months on sick leave because of an illness or medical procedure, you can talk to Occupational Health or Human Resources (or your manager) about a phased return to work. This usually would mean a spell of part-time work, a lighter workload, working from home, or a mixture of all three – and makes it very much easier to slide back into your working role. It's an increasingly common approach, because employers have found it works, and it makes the transition from sofa to desk much more likely to succeed. Employers prefer this to someone coming back full-time too early, and just ending up off sick again or, alternatively, staying off for a longer time than necessary, just to be sure.

Returning after maternity leave

Picking up where you left off after maternity leave can pose its own anxieties, more so if it's been several months or more. There is a feeling out there that new mothers may have what's become known as 'baby brain' or 'mummy brain', and this can sap your confidence when you're faced with an important team meeting on your first day back. Will you manage to string a sensible sentence together? How have things moved on? Here are some thoughts new mothers may find helpful:

1. **There is unlikely to have been a change in your brain power**. This would be very unusual. What is most likely is that looking after one or more small children requires a different sort of brain use. You have to juggle lots of information and needs all day, and attend to multiple physical and practical tasks, sometimes without a break and with the effects of grazing for food and sleep deprivation thrown into the mix. With a first baby, everything can be new, so you also have to learn a whole new way of life, and learn it fast. Nothing is predictable and speedy decision making is constantly required. In other words, your brain can become overloaded. Little wonder then that you can find yourself stumbling for a name or a phone number, or giving the cat the baby's lunch. As you become more used to motherhood and have fewer disturbed nights, things should return to normal.

2. **Your work-based skills and knowledge are still there**. They just need dusting off, refreshing and using again. Just like your work clothes.

3. **Your organisational and practical skills will have been enhanced**, along with your stamina and time management, and your softer skills, such as empathy and communication.

4. **You're likely to have made friendships that can last a lifetime** with other new mothers and parents. These will provide support and companionship, and will strengthen your resilience for years ahead. My children are grown up now, but some of my best and closest friends are still some of the parents I met when my children were tiny, including colleagues who were juggling work with the responsibilities of young children, just as I was.

5. **If you can, join colleagues for nights out**, while you're on maternity leave, or just meet up for coffee now and then – this is an enjoyable way to stay in touch, maintain friendships and have a chance to rehearse your workplace role and keep it fresh.

6. **Be like a 'Transformer' toy**. When you start back at work, before opening the door to your workplace, try spending a few moments mentally transforming yourself from 'mum' to who you are in your job. Even after settling back into work, I found the drive from home to work was a great time for me to change hats and switch the professional me back on.

7. **Work can seem like a dawdle** after handling a child and a home 24 hours a day. Your job can be a welcome break from the 'extreme multitasking', quick-fire decision making and constant interruptions that is a day at home with the children – although your job may require you to do this, too!

8. **At work, you'll have more quality time to concentrate** and to think about your responses in meetings. Likewise, for your

e-mails, in your dealings with an employee or your manager, or your input to a project. The joy of an unbroken thought train will return to your day. And you'll have the wonderful benefit of an undisturbed meal break.

> *But the problem is that when I go around and speak on campuses, I still don't get young men standing up and saying, How can I combine career and family?*
>
> **Gertrude Stein, American art collector and writer, 1874–1946**

Does your work sometimes make you angry?

The frustrations and stresses of the workplace can build and build, like a tap dripping inside you until, one day, for no particular reason, it can suddenly overflow and surface as anger, a tantrum or, worse, violence. It wouldn't be the first time that such anger has led to an office or desk being trashed. For others, the anger simmers away quietly, surfacing often in the form of general irritability and impatience with others, sarcasm, sulking, put-downs, not listening, being obstructive or argumentative, or aggressive behaviour.

Sometimes anger can stay deep within the person, never surfacing, but instead slowly turning on themselves, and producing a feeling of personal despair or even depression. This can happen through choice, or because of the power situation you are working in. And, because it is often more socially acceptable for a man to show irritability and anger than a woman, this can be more of a problem for women. Many men find an outlet for such feelings through contact sports such as rugby or football, or through computer games, golf or squash.

Coping with your own anger

So, it is essential to do something about angry feelings. They can't just be left to sort themselves out. But, contrary to much of the advice on this, it isn't about expressing it whenever we feel it, or about hitting a punch bag. There is lots of evidence suggesting that, if you express your anger, it can grow and become even more damaging. It is an emotional response very similar to the 'fight, flight or freeze' response, and is fuelled by the 'fight' part of the equation. That's why, when faced with a situation at work that makes you angry or frustrated, you might want to walk out and slam a door (flight), feel so angry you can't move or speak (freeze), or feel like shouting, throwing or hitting something (fight). So, what do you do? Well, just like for a panic attack, the answer is to use relaxation to take the emotional response away.

But, before I explain more about that, there is so much you can do to *prevent feelings of frustration and anger arising in the first place*, and we've already covered these in earlier chapters. You can:

➡ use assertiveness techniques to deal with others, so that you are much less likely to feel angry or frustrated (Chapters 3, 4 and 5);

➡ avoid problematic situations arising through good communication skills (Chapter 6).

But, *if you do find yourself feeling angry,* here are some practical suggestions on how to deal with this emotion safely at the time, instead of bottling it all up or expressing it in unhelpful ways. Try these next time you feel angry:

➡ As soon as you feel you are becoming angry, use any relaxation or breathing technique we've covered and that works for you – this will help to diffuse the anger.

➡ As you feel anger coming on, challenge and question the angry thoughts you're having (as we did in Chapter 2): What is the evidence for what you are thinking? Is there another explanation? Are you jumping to conclusions? Are you ignoring the positive? Ask yourself, Is it really worth getting angry about?

➡ If nothing works, make your excuses and leave the situation, then use relaxation until you feel calmer, or release the negative energy constructively by doing something physically demanding and useful like going for a run or a brisk walk.

In short

➡ All stress is bad for you, even a little bit.

➡ Stress produces a range of different symptoms affecting mind, body and behaviour.

➡ There are many reasons for feeling stressed at work.

➡ You can sometimes do something about the cause of stress, but the best way to combat stress is to make yourself more resilient to it using straightforward techniques and lifestyle changes.

➡ Using some form of relaxation every day can reduce the effects of stress.

➡ Breathing techniques can work very quickly.   ▶

- ➡ There is a temptation to work through breaks, but this is not helpful at all.
- ➡ Even 'happy' events can be stressful because of the changes and extra demands they can bring.
- ➡ Stress can produce attacks of panic or anxiety lasting 20 minutes or so. Using a relaxation technique can help to disperse the panic.
- ➡ You can relax your mind using a range of techniques, including mindfulness.
- ➡ Relaxation can also diffuse anger.

Chapter eight

Keep going and stay confident

What you'll do in this chapter:	This will help you to be more confident in any work situation, especially:
1. Find ways to maintain your confidence and motivation throughout your career.	1. When your motivation weakens.
	2. If your confidence fades.
2. Find ways to make plans and reach your goals.	3. When you've had a disappointing event or missed out on a job or promotion.
3. Find ways to get over setbacks and move on.	
4. Discover how your personal journal can help.	4. For goal setting and career planning.

This is the closing chapter and I'm nearing the end of the book. In this chapter, I want to give you the skills to maintain your self-confidence and keep it in good order for any eventuality, because you have to play the long game at work. You have to stay fit for purpose and that means maintaining staying power and resilience. That way you'll stay a step ahead and be ready for anything that's thrown at you. You'll be on top of your work and find it so much more satisfying, meaning that you can enjoy life more, too.

Staying on track

Even when you've worked out your goals for the way ahead, it can be so easy to be distracted from the simplest of plans. Even finding the time and energy can become impossible. But, even in the busiest life, there is so much you can still do to stay on track, if it's truly what you want. Regrets later in life are so much harder to deal with than finding ways to keep your show on the road now.

Here are some straightforward strategies that can help you stay with your plan, keep your energy levels high, and reach your goals.

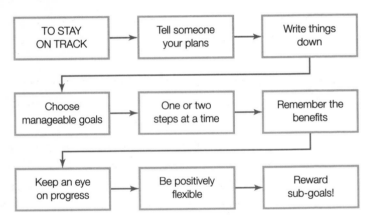

Super strategies for reaching your goals

1. **Tell someone your plans**. Tell someone you trust about your plans. That way, they'll ask you about them, making you more likely to make progress. Or, find a positive and encouraging friend who has time to be your coach or mentor and give you support and encouragement.

2. **Write down your plans.** Keep your plans in your personal journal (or whatever you prefer) and make this your route map. You can set up your electronic devices to flag up your targets.

3. **Choose realistic and manageable targets**. Decide on real manageable targets, rather than having vague general ideas or aims that are beyond your reach. Choose realistic and achievable aims and outcomes. Use a SWOT analysis (think about Strengths, Weaknesses, Opportunities, Threats), or anything else you're familiar with, to see the full picture before choosing targets.

4. **One or two steps at a time**. Keep your eye on the overall plan, but take on just one or two items at a time. Don't take on more than you can cope with.

5. **Remember why you're doing this**. Remember the expected benefits and disappearing negatives. Note down all the benefits you (or others) will gain from your plans, and all the negatives that will disappear when you achieve them. Read these often.

6. **Monitor progress.** Check your progress at the same time every week or every month, at a time you know you're most likely to have space in your schedule.

7. **Be positively flexible.** Don't dwell on negative experiences. Everyone has them. See them as just another part of the overall process. Take stock and move on. If something isn't working, try something else. Be ready for change.

8. **Make it worth it.** Pick out rewards for yourself for each sub-goal reached successfully, with a special reward chosen for when a major aim is achieved.

Setbacks happen – but you can get over them

There are no secrets to success. It is the result of preparation, hard work, and learning from failure.

Colin Powell, former United States Secretary of State, b. 1937

One day everything just slots into place, whilst on other days you can be all fingers and thumbs and do nothing right. But the bad day soon passes, to be replaced by a number of better, more hopeful and more useful, days when you can take another step forward and feel more positive. Setbacks happen to everyone. They are so common as to be considered a standard part of life. So much so that you'll be less fazed and cope much better with a setback if you expect this to happen somewhere along the line and know that it's not all down to you. Any number of outside circumstances can bring about a setback for you, and then there are the slip-ups and mistakes we all make for ourselves because we're human. All this is part and parcel of the learning process and of life itself. Just make sure that you don't give up, but keep trying and stay on track.

What you can do

1. **Build setbacks into your plans**. Be ready for success and achievement, but be ready for a disappointment and a setback, too. Both happen to us all.

2. **Keep your plans flexible** and keep your options open. There is no point in setting yourself up to fail.

3. **Don't just have rewards for successes**, work out ways to reinvigorate and pick yourself up after a setback. Try a motivational course, a networking event, a short course, or a retreat.

4. **Don't always blame yourself**. Our plans are often spoilt by 'circumstances beyond our control' which are nothing to do with us. It most certainly won't always be just down to you.

5. **Ask for some feedback**. If you don't get a job or promotion, or an appraisal has been a concern, or whatever it is that you feel is a disappointment or a setback, don't just go away and

lick your wounds, ruminating on what's wrong with you, or why these things always happen to you – and then decide not to try again. Find out more about what has happened and why from those concerned. This is considered quite usual in these circumstances and you can find out things that will help you to improve and move forward.

6. **Have your own debrief** if the setback has involved just you. Think things through, decide what went wrong and why, and decide what to learn from it to take forward. If others were involved, get together for a joint debrief. There's so much to learn from this to make success another day much more likely.

7. **Have lots of ideas**. Thomas Edison, who developed the first electric light bulb in 1880 said, 'If you want to have a good idea, have a lot of them.' Most entrepreneurs will tell you the same. Many of their ideas don't work out – but it takes only one idea to produce a major success – so don't be afraid to try and fail. Every successful person will have done this, too.

8. **Consider having a mentor**, life or business coach to support, encourage and motivate you, and be there as an objective sounding board.

Chill time

Breathing by numbers

1. Count how many times you breathe out in a minute.

2. Now, do the same thing again.

3. The second number should be lower than the first and you should now feel more relaxed.

Keep on with your personal journal

I hope you've been making some use of your personal journal, which was introduced at the beginning of the book. Great, if you have. But not a problem if you haven't, or you're just dipping in to the book here and there. It's never too late. You can easily pick up on it now, or even after you've read the whole book.

Wherever you are on this, here's a review of the ways I introduced for using a personal journal:

1. **Make a short note describing your day** (or longer if you want to) each evening or first thing next morning. You can use a single word or phrase, such as good, OK, more positive today, disappointing or fair. Or maybe use an appropriate 'smiley' (or 'emoticon') instead. If numbers appeal more, just score your day on 1 to 10 or 1 to 100. When you look back over these notes, it really helps you to see where the good days and bad days were and, if cross-referenced with your work and home diary, you'll maybe see reasons for these. Sometimes this can show that maybe you've had more good days than you thought. It's so easy to remember only the tough days.

2. **Write down three good or positive things that happened each day.** At the end of each day, take a few moments to think back over the day. It need not be anything major. Start with every day to get the idea, then maybe three or four times a week. Studies show this can alter your mindset for the better.

3. **Keep a note of the really useful stuff.** Go right to the back of your journal and start a new page by writing a heading at the top, 'Useful stuff' (or any other title you prefer). As you work through the book, when you find a particularly helpful idea, thought or explanation, you can make a short note of this, along with the page it was on.

4. **New stuff to use *now*, *soon*, or *later***. I also suggested that you make up three lists on three separate pages, as you work through the book. Put these somewhere easy to find, maybe at the back or centre of your journal. Here are the headings for your three lists:

   1. Changes and techniques you're starting *now*.

   2. Changes and techniques you want to start *soon*.

   3. Changes and techniques that you'll get to work on *later*.

   So, as time progresses, you can move items around as they move from *soon* to *now*, or from *later* to *soon*. If you are using an electronic journal, a quick cut and paste will do it. If you're on paper, using small 'stickies' on each page, means you can move them around easily, too. You can make a start to this now, if you haven't done this yet. It really helps you stay on track.

My top 10 confidence boosters

1. **Never forget your strengths** and don't be too hard on yourself. Keep a list of all the things you're good at, for your eyes only. Be honest, but not modest. They don't need to be huge things: keeping a tidy desk, sticking at things, good memory, and so on. Read the list every week, and add to it whenever you can. No one's perfect. We all make mistakes. It's not always your fault, either – it's often someone else to blame.

2. **Look after your health**. Fully fit, you can achieve so much. Regular enjoyable exercise builds stamina, strength and resilience. Eat a healthy diet and get your sleep. Make breaks, leisure and relaxation part of your week and part of your everyday routine, just like brushing your teeth. Enjoy looking good and making the most of yourself. People will reflect the good feeling back to you.

3. **Be calm** and cushion yourself from stress. Avoid hurrying and rushing. Build and maintain your resilience against stress. Simple relaxation and stress management techniques will calm your body and mind and can be a lifesaver. Relax every day, even if it's just for five minutes. Use mindfulness for at least a minute at some point every day. Those few minutes will pay you back handsomely.

4. **Remember you have rights** as a human being, and they apply in the workplace, too. Here are just some of them: you have the right to your own opinion, to be treated with respect and as an equal, not to be bullied or put down, to be listened to, to fail, to make mistakes, to try again.

5. **Behave assertively** (not aggressively). Respect your own needs and those of others, know how to compromise and say no when you want to. Where there is disagreement or conflict, be prepared and ready to negotiate or compromise. Whenever possible, aim for a 'win-win'.

6. **Plan, prioritise and organise** – know where you are, where you want to go and how you plan to get there. Be sure of what you want. Think about and plan this carefully. Decide on your first step and act on it. Be ready to adapt your plan as and when needed. Whatever the task ahead, prepare for it. Practise, too, if it's relevant, e.g. a presentation. Spend real quality time doing this, as this will up your game as well as bolster your confidence and self-esteem.

7. **Body language**. Walk confident and talk confident and you'll look and feel more confident. Head up, shoulders and body relaxed, making regular eye contact. Open a door confidently as you come into a room and make an entrance. Open posture, firm handshake and warm calm voice show you're happy for people to come and talk to you. Speak clearly, with rhythm, enthusiasm and momentum. Add passion, too, if you have it, and charisma may follow!

8. **Write things down**, like your plans and targets. And keep using your personal journal. Make it into what you want it to be and what works for you.

9. **Visualise**. Create a video in your mind's eye of the situation you want to deal with more confidently. Make this as clear as you can manage and go through it frame by frame, dealing with it successfully and coping with any difficulties.

10. **Regularly review** how things are going. What went well? What wasn't so good? Decide what you want to take forward. Take forward what is working. Be flexible and ready for change. Onwards and upwards.

IN THE ZONE

You can boost your confidence by being more pro-active, by taking action and by putting energy into everything you do. Over analysing and endless ruminating just wastes valuable time and energy. It doesn't need to be stunning, spectacular or spot on. Just doing enough, making a fair effort or taking a sensible stab at it will always beat doing nothing, hands down.

A few words to finish

Continuous effort, not intelligence or strength, is the key to unlocking our potential.

Winston Churchill, British Prime Minister, 1874–1965

So, there you have it. It's all there for the taking. And it's all about putting in the effort and keeping going. You can also refer back to these confidence boosters at any time, or to any other part of the book. But, whatever you do, don't go straight out and use what you've learned to resolve your biggest, most sensitive or delicate problems. You need to practise many of the skills we've talked about, before letting them loose. Take these new skills on board one at a time, try them out in low-key everyday situations to become comfortable with them, and then you'll be ready for the off, when the time is right. This is just a starting point and I've given you a springboard for change. I wish you fantastic success and achievements with your new skills and enhanced confidence.

In short

→ Reading this book is not an end in itself; it is your springboard for improved self-confidence at work.

→ You're more likely to achieve the outcomes you want if you choose realistic goals, write down your plans, work to a manageable timescale, keep an eye on progress and on the benefits you'll gain.

→ Maintaining confidence is easier if you are flexible in your approach, and ready to change your goals if something doesn't work out.

→ Don't be fazed by setbacks and disappointments, as they happen to everyone, and they are not always your fault. A setback always shows you ways to make success more likely.

→ It's better to tackle low-key events or situations first, before moving on to the more sensitive, delicate areas of your work.

→ If returning to work after a break, cut yourself some slack and allow time to come back up to speed. There are ways to make the transition easier.

→ Many people find that having a mentor or coach increases their motivation and self-confidence.

→ There are many simple and effective ways you can improve your all-round self-confidence, including keeping a personal journal (see the list of confidence boosters, earlier).

Appendix 1: Useful contacts

Association for Coaching
www.associationforcoaching.com

Centre for Mindfulness Research and Practice, Bangor University
www.bangor.ac.uk/mindfulness/
E-mail: mindfulness@bangor.ac.uk

Chartered Institute of Personnel and Development (CIPD)
www.cipd.co.uk
Wide-ranging information to help you in your work and study.

Coaching Division of BACP (British Association for Counselling and Psychotherapy)

www.bacpcoaching.co.uk

The Coaching & Mentoring Network
www.coachingnetwork.org.uk

Health and Safety Executive (HSE)
www.hse.gov.uk

International Stress Management Association
www.isma.org.uk

Bully Online
www.bullyonline.org
The world's largest resource on workplace bullying and related issues.

Government services and information
www.gov.uk
Wide-ranging information on government policies, announcements, publications, statistics and consultations.

Job Stress Network
www.workhealth.org

The UK National Work–stress Network
www.workstress.net

Appendix 2:
Hint for Chapter 2 – flipping cube activity

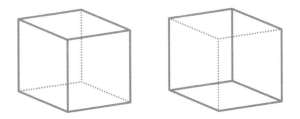

Index

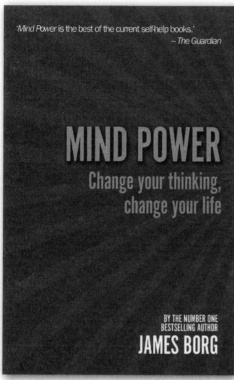

21/01/14

Be more, achieve more and stress less – mindfulness can change how you work.

mindfulness
for busy people

turning
FRANTIC AND FRAZZLED
into
calm and composed

Michael Sinclair
and Josie Seydel

9781292004501

Mindfulness for Busy People will show you how to apply the transformative power of mindfulness to your busy working life, helping you to de-stress, find your own unique space of calm, and ready yourself for whatever challenges you face.

Available from all good bookshops

eBOOK
also available